START YOUR OWN
NEWSLETTER
PUBLISHING BUSINESS

START YOUR OWN
NEWSLETTER PUBLISHING BUSINESS

Extra Income Magazine
National Business Library

Scott, Foresman and Company
Glenview, Illinois   London

ISBN 0-673-46342-7

1 2 3 4 5 6 RRC 95 94 93 92 91 90

Library of Congress Cataloging in Publication Data

Start Your Own Newsletter Publishing Business / National
Business Library.
      p.   cm.
Includes bibliographical references.
ISBN 0–673–46342–7
1. Newsletters—Publishing.　I. National Business Library.

Notice of Liability

The information in this book is distributed on an "As Is" basis, without warranty. Neither the author nor Scott, Foresman and Company shall have any liablility to the customer or any other person or entity with respect to any liability, loss, or damage caused or alleged to be caused directly or indirectly by the content contained herein.

Dear Friend,

I would personally like to extend my congratulations to you on taking the first all-important step in making your dream of owning your own business a reality.

Start Your Own Newsletter Publishing Business is the result of many hours of in-depth research into the Newsletter Publishing industry. Our exclusive team of professional business writers have brought years of practical experience to this project and we know that the information provided in this book will set you on the road to success.

Owning your own business can be the most exciting and rewarding venture you will ever experience. We talk to hundreds of small business owners who make comments like, "Doing something I really enjoy makes every new day a pleasure," or "If I had known I could be realizing this kind of income, rather than making my former boss wealthy, I would have started my own business years ago."

It's true! You'll never get rich working for someone else. By capitalizing on your experience, investing time and energy, and studying the proven techniques and business methods provided in this book, you will be well on the way to realizing your goals for success in your own venture. It takes courage to begin. Without a doubt, the first step is the hardest—and you have already taken it!

Sincerely,

James J. Maher
Publisher

P.S. Please let me know when you have established your new business. I look forward to congratulating you again! If yours is an interesting or unique new business story, we may include it in our series as we have done for hundreds of others.

Acknowledgments

The project editor on this book was Diane Beausoleil. The cover was designed by Interface Studio, and the text design was developed by BMR, Inc. Lisa Labrecque was project manager. The book was made into pages by BMR using Pagemaker 3 on the Macintosh. The text type is Palatino and Helvetica condensed. The entire project was coordinated by Gene Schwartz of Consortium House, Ltd., Del Mar, California. This book was printed and bound by R. R. Donnelley.

Start Your Own
Newsletter Publishing Business

Table of Contents

Introduction

Profits in Publishing

The newsletter business is booming! It is estimated that gross revenues from newsletters are currently over two billion dollars per year in this country ... and growing.

One reason for this phenomenon is that newsletters are a fun, relatively simply, and inexpensive way to start a business. Newslettters provide a service, satisfy your urge to be a publisher, and can be started as a part-time business ... you can continue working in a regular job to cover expenses until your subscription base warrants pursuing it full-time.

With careful planning and development, it should be possible to create a very healthy income by becoming a newsletter publisher. We spoke with people who are grossing $25,000 a year with a small, four-page newsletter that they produce in their spare time, and others who are realizing gross income of $150,000 with financial newsletters that cost as much as $500 per year for a single subscription.

Basic start-up requirements are a typewriter or computer, and a topic. You will require cash flow to pay for advertising, reproduction of the newsletter, and mailing expenses until the subscriptions start rolling in.

As for publishing or journalism experience, it certainly helps make the job easier. However, if you have a strong topic and a basic ability to organize information, this is one opportunity where you can learn while you earn. Just be sure to read and study as many newsletters as you can get your hands on, and don't be afraid to take creative risks in making yours better.

You certainly must have expertise—or at bare minimum, a healthy interest—in the specific topic you are planning to build the newsletter around. And although there are thousands of newsletters being published in this country, there is always a market for a fresh approach to an old idea.

As your paper bonanza starts to grow, keep an eye on your production goals and on the quality of your newsletter. Soon you will join the ranks of newsletter publishers who enjoy status of experts in their field . . . not to mention the pleasure they get from their share of the billings being made in this lucrative business.

By reading this business guide and following the suggestions outlined, it is conceivable that you could have your newsletter publishing business up and running within a few month's time. Good luck! ■

1

The Growth of Small Business

The 1980s have been referred to as America's "entrepreneurial era." In 1985, there were 500,000 new business startups in this country, but in the following year that number increased to an incredible 750,000. Last year, more than one million new businesses were started in this country—with almost half by women—and this figure is expected to rise dramatically during the early 1990s.

More and more people are opting to leave their 9-to-5 jobs and stop "making someone else rich" to focus their energies on building a successful business of their own. For these people, it is no longer enough to spend nearly three-quarters of their lives working in a dead-end job, putting up with petty office politics, unappreciative employers and wasting time on long commutes just to bring home headaches and a small paycheck.

You can never be too young, too old, too busy or too poor to start a business.

Today, the number of individuals who are self-employed is at its highest level ever and, based on your decision to study this business guide, it is quite possible that you will be joining the ranks of small business owners in the near future. It may be simply a dream at this moment, but that is how it starts.

Starting and operating your own small business is one of the most exciting and satisfying challenges you can undertake. There are no limitations on income potential when you are investing time and energy in your own enterprise. With the practical information provided in this guide and dedication to your business goals, your chances for success are excellent.

What *is* a "Small Business"?

The majority of businesses in the U.S. today are classified as small businesses. The definitions of what constitutes a small business run the gamut from fewer than 500 employees to various indicators of annual assets or sales volumes. However, in this book, small business is defined as one which is independently owned and operated.

The major benefit of this type of business is that you have the ability to make decisions quickly and act on them immediately; something that typically bogs down big businesses because of the number of people involved in the decision-making process. The other advantages include the fact that small businesses can provide personalized service to the community or the market they are serving and that the owner has the freedom, the independence and the control to operate exactly as he or she chooses.

It is still important to remember, however, that most major corporations, from Ford Motor Company and McDonald's to Mary Kay Cosmetics, started out as small businesses, as dreams. It was because of basic business sense and a willingness to learn and adapt as their companies grew that Henry Ford, Ray Kroc and Mary Kay, and thousands like them, steered their dreams into monumental financial successes.

Whether your goal is to operate a solely owned home-based business from your garage, the kitchen table, or a spare bedroom that supplements an existing income, or to start a business venture that involves raising substantial capital, finding and setting up a commercial location and hiring employees, you have the potential to enjoy an independent lifestyle that carries with it a number of rewards.

Entrepreneur
A person who undertakes an independent enterprise; one who has made the decision to go into business for him/herself.

Accepting the Challenge

However, these rewards do not come without hard work and the willingness to research and understand all facets of running your business. Many new businesses fail within the first few years.

Reasons given for the early demise of a small business invariably include comments from the owners pertaining to undercapitalization, misunderstanding of the importance of advertising, confusion about pricing products or services and a lack of knowledge in areas of financial planning and day-to-day operating techniques.

It isn't that someone purposely starts a business without having explored these areas. However, many times a person feels that because they have been a good woodworker, computer operator, salesperson, or any other specialist, while working for someone else, they can easily transfer their expertise into their own business. This is only partially true.

While it is imperative that you have these certain skills or talents—because selling them is what your ultimate success will be based upon—it is equally important to understand *how* to sell them, how to recognize whether you are *really* making money or not, and what steps to take to ensure the continued growth of your business.

Sounds easy, right? It really can be. But like anything else worth doing, starting your own business means careful planning. You wouldn't consider taking a month-long vacation without doing some serious planning to ensure that the house was taken care of while you were gone, that you had made reservations for lodging, tours and flights, and converted your cash into traveler's checks, etc.

There are so many aspects involved with running a business, it is vital to be prepared for any eventuality, and being prepared comes, quite simply, from being informed, so that when situations do arise, you know how to deal with them.

Is "Failure" Really Failure?

We have all heard stories about people who started their businesses on a "shoestring" with little more than a wing and a prayer and were successful because of their sheer determination to make it work. It does happen, but these people are the exception rather than the rule, and in most cases have had experts standing behind them to give them guidance when problems come up. Others do fail and, unfortunately, this is a factor that often holds potential new business owners back. We hear and read amazingly high figures related to business failure.

A recent survey conducted by a New York-based business consulting firm indicated that many people, including small business owners, believe that up to ninety percent of all new companies fail within their first year. This is simply not true.

According to an on-going research project conducted by Albert Shapero, Professor of the American Free Enterprise System at Ohio State University for many years, no one really knows the true failure rate of new business. The main reason for this is because there is not really a standard definition of "failure" in this case. He points out that a number of businesses close for a variety of reasons that are rarely documented.

For example, in some cases the owners reach retirement age and have no one to pass the business along to; others shut down because the owners simply get bored; while some entrepreneurs will file a Chapter 11 bankruptcy, which basically gives them the opportunity to stay in business and continue operating under a court-approved plan even though they become a statistic on the "failure" list.

The other extremely important aspect to consider when thinking about the benefits and risks of starting your own business is that having a business fail has never been a deterrent for true entrepreneurs. Many well-known business moguls failed at least once, and often more than once, before striking it rich.

Learning from Experience

In fact, almost anyone who has had a business fail will tell you that what they learned from the experience was more valuable than anything they could have been taught in a business school, and provided them with the knowledge they needed to start another venture successfully. This kind of determination is a valid qualification for self-employment and will certainly pay off handsomely.

When you own your own business, you are generally chief cook and bottle-washer. There will be times, such as when your accounts receivable are running 60 days late, or the phone company puts the wrong number in your Yellow Page listing, when returning to the world of 9-to-5 will seem like a viable option.

This is where self-discipline, an unwavering belief in your product or service, and the determination to be your own boss will pull you through. But, again, we can't stress enough the importance of planning, understanding basic business practices, being aware of consumer trends, and taking the time to develop, implement, and update goals to ensure success for your efforts.

Inside This Book

This book is designed to provide you with the details you will need to start your newsletter publishing business, techniques to help you with day-to-day operations, and actual case histories of people just like you who had a dream and, through planning and determination, were able to turn it into a successful reality.

In addition to focusing on aspects of business, we cover important business matters ranging from the entrepreneurial profile and our exclusive Entrepreneurial Quiz, how to find the right audience for your business through easy marketing techniques and organizing for efficiency, to legalities, financial concerns, how to easily start your business at home, and methods for charting growth.

You will find specific how-to information on advertising and promoting your business, finding capital, saving money on operating expenses, and developing a simple bookkeeping system that will show you, at a glance, whether you are facing a financial crisis or realizing a profit.

You're never too young, too old, too busy, or too poor to start a business. Owning your own business means taking advantage of our marvelous system of free enterprise. Earning a substantial living and, even better, realizing a profit for doing something you enjoy is the American dream come true.

The road to financial independence through self-employment is challenging and rewarding. The opportunities for entrepreneurs have never been better. Armed with a solid product or service to sell, the determination to succeed and, most important, business know-how, there is nothing that can stand in your way. ■

Notes

Key Points

_____

_____

_____

Personal Thoughts

_____

_____

_____

_____

_____

Additional Research

_____

_____

_____

_____

2

The Entrepreneurial Profile

Starting a business is one thing; making it work is another. Success in self-employment is largely the result of careful planning and the understanding of basic business techniques and formulas.

Start a business based on your expertise in a specific field and focus your involvement in an area that you thoroughly enjoy. As many successful entrepreneurs claim, making money doing something you love is the best way to ensure a profitable future. Addressing inevitable business challenges with creating a product or providing a service is easier when it gives you a sense of pleasure and personal satisfaction.

Personality is also a factor in determining what kind of business to get involved in, the way you will eventually set up the legal structure (sole proprietorship, partnership, etc.) and how you will run the business on a day-to-day basis. For example, if you are planning to start a business which is based on your artistic or creative abilities, it is possible that your personality is not suited to the very important aspect of sales. But without strong selling abilities there is a likelihood that your goal of distributing nationally, for example, your hand-carved wooden boxes will not come to fruition.

This is not to say that you should decide against going into business for yourself. It simply indicates that it would be in your best interest to join forces with someone who *does* have strong selling skills, who believes in the product as much as you do and will work toward a common goal.

On the other hand, if your personality is geared to working with people, consider a business that will emphasize this ability, such as developing seminars or workshops based on your area of expertise, providing independent counseling or tutoring, or a service such as desktop publishing, which depends on your interaction with people on a one-to-one or a group basis for success.

Ten Positive Entrepreneurial Traits

1. Motivation
2. Confidence
3. Self-awareness
4. Courage
5. Knowledge

6. Optimism
7. Experience
8. Decisiveness
9. Patience
10. Drive

Self-motivation, otherwise known as drive, is one of the most important personality traits of successful entrepreneurs. This is the characteristic that gets you going and keeps you moving when you are in business for yourself. It's what helps you to keep turning out those wooden boxes, upgrading your technical skills or develop new and improved promotional techniques when business is slow. It's what gives you the tenacity and confidence to call on a potential client even though they have told you 'No' three times.

Self-motivation is also what helps you to overcome the fears and concerns that inevitably arise when you own your own business. It is the main ingredient which has spurred on those people we hear about who have achieved success despite drawbacks, such as minimal capital, lack of education, or limited experience.

People with a high degree of self-motivation see the greatest obstacles, such as learning a new aspect of business management, as new and exciting challenges to be overcome. If you have ever undertaken a project without fully understanding the mechanics involved in performing the task or knowing what the outcome would be, you were operating on self-motivation—the conviction that you would be able to learn whatever was needed to accomplish your goal.

And regardless of the outcome of the project, you undoubtedly gained more experience and knowledge than you had before, which only works to increase your sense of motivation to handle new challenges.

Research shows that to be able to address the many and varied situations that arise in business ownership, the true entrepreneur should possess the following kinds of personality traits:

The willingness to take risks. Courage is a valuable trait when striving for success. We have heard successful people say something similar to this, "I don't know how I did it, I just made a phone call and asked for the money I needed." It was more than luck that made it possible for this person to raise the capital they needed to get their business off the ground; it was the willingness to take a chance—in this case, the risk that they would receive a negative response to the request.

The owner of a small cabinet-refinishing business said, "I always figure that the worst thing that can happen is someone will say no, so it never hurts to try." In the game of business, you must be willing to take chances. Even if you don't get exactly what you want every time, the odds are good that if you feel strongly about what you need, you will get it. But you have to ask!

Confidence. The age-old philosophy of positive thinking is a step in the direction of success. By behaving as if you already are a success at what you do, it follows that you will be, and your customers will believe it, too. A confident attitude is one of the most appealing traits you can exhibit to a prospective client, for it lets them know that they will be getting the best their money can buy.

Patience.   When you own your own business, there will be moments when you feel like the roof is caving in, especially when your suppliers seem to be taking their own sweet time in fulfilling an important order, or when a customer's demands seem to be unrealistic. Although you may be able to hurry the supplier along a little bit, you must remember that your customers are always right, since they are the ones who can financially make or break your business.

If you are aware that patience is not your strong suit, develop a stop-gap exercise for yourself to use at times when coping is a definite necessity. Whether it's the time-honored 'count to ten before saying a word' theory, visualizing a pleasant scene, or repeating a secret phrase to yourself when tension is running high, it will be to your advantage.

You have to accept whatever comes,
and the important thing is
that you meet it with courage
and with the best you have to give.

Eleanor Roosevelt

Decision-making.   Business has been described as a process of one decision after another. Often, a decision has to be made on the spur-of-the-moment. In those instances, you should go with your intuition and trust that you are doing the right thing.

However, if you are the type of person who prefers to analyze your options, weigh all the factors and make decisions slowly, then this is what you must do. It will not only keep your confidence intact, but will ensure that you are taking the correct action. Again, careful planning will help you predict many of the decision-making situations that arise in business. As time goes by and you grow more comfortable in your role as business owner, you will undoubtedly find yourself making decisions more quickly.

Experience. The results of a Dun & Bradstreet survey conducted a few years back indicated that a primary reason that some businesses fail within a few years after start-up was 'incompetence in the area of business experience.' Whether or not your experience is directly related to the business you are planning to start, it is an essential component for growth.

If you feel you do not have enough business experience, there are several avenues you can take before starting your own enterprise. Returning to school for specialized courses is one answer. Most community colleges and adult education facilities offer classes and seminars in business start-up and maintenance. There are also hundreds of courses available to you by mail—over 1,200 schools and universities now offer home study or correspondence courses which will, in many cases, give you official certification in your field.

However, your best solution is to take a job in the field you are interested in. By asking questions about all aspects of the business, you will gain experience, be getting paid for learning, and find out whether this is really what you want to do—before sinking money, time, and energy into the enterprise.

Perseverance. One of the adages you will hear time and time again when talking to entrepreneurs is that perseverance is ninety percent of the battle to succeed. If you are like the majority of new small business owners, the entire staff and support system for your venture is probably *you*. Making a dream come true can be a lonely task, especially when you are just getting started, and ensuring that it works often means little rest and relaxation. You must be willing to persevere during the rough times, to hang in there during the slow periods, and to maintain your belief in your product and service even when it seems like no one else in the world knows you exist. It has been written that by perseverance, the snail reached the ark. So it is with success!

The Entrepreneurial "A to Z" Appraisal

Owning a business calls for the ability to handle many different situations with confidence. The following self-appraisal quiz has no right or wrong answers. It is designed to help you in determining personality traits, attitudes and qualifications which will benefit you in your venture.

Use the letters "S" for strong or "N" for needs improvement beside the characteristics listed below. Give yourself sufficient time to analyze each trait. Upon completion, use the appraisal as a starting point for discussions with friends and family members about your business profile. Acknowledging your strong and weak points will help you prepare for your role as an entrepreneur.

Achievement. I have a strong desire to be successful in my chosen business venture. _____

Belief. I have faith in myself and the service or product I am specializing in to build my business. _____

Creativity. I am able to address situations in imaginative and innovative ways to reach my goals. _____

Discipline. I am self-motivated and able to handle necessary tasks, whether or not I enjoy them. _____

Efficient. I am organized and able to arrange my priorities or change my work methods as needed for maximum production. _____

Friendly. I am genuinely interested in people and enjoy my interactions with them on a day-to-day basis. _____

Goal-oriented. I have a tendency to set my sights on pre-set goals and to work hard toward them. _____

Health-conscious. I am aware of my physical abilities and have the insight to work smart in order to preserve my health. _____

Independent. I am able to work alone, if necessary, and prefer to be responsible for my own actions. _____

Judgment. My conclusions about people or situations are generally accurate. _____

Knowledge. I have solid experience in my field and have spent enough time in a professional business setting to learn the ropes. _____

Leadership. I am able to direct people effectively while instilling confidence and loyalty. _____

Maturity. I am willing to work toward long-term goals and do not get upset by the inevitable minor set-backs. _____

Networking. I have, or am willing to develop, associations with other entrepreneurs for support in my venture. _____

Optimism. I am able to see what is right about a situation and to explore its potential to the fullest. _____

Positive attitude. I am convinced that I can accomplish anything I set my mind to doing and rarely entertain negative thoughts. _____

Questioning. I am not afraid to ask questions to get the information I need to expand my knowledge. _____

Resourceful. I am able to find ways to accomplish just about any task I must do. _____

Sales ability. I can present information about myself and my business in a convincing and honest manner.   _____

Tolerance. I am able to handle stressful situations with a positive and realistic attitude.   _____

Undaunted spirit. I am unafraid of the unknown. In fact, I enjoy a challenge and accept the consequences of my actions.   _____

Venturesome. I am not afraid of hard work to reach my goals and enjoy finding new, positive ways to handle troublesome situations.   _____

Well-balanced. I generally maintain a sense of humor when things don't work out as expected.   _____

eXpressive. I am able to express ideas and feelings, both orally and in writing, clearly and logically.   _____

Youthful nature. I am capable of tackling work with enthusiasm and a high level of energy.   _____

Zest. I look forward to enjoying my business, the people I will be dealing with, and the resulting fruits of my labor.   _____

Although this is not a test, merely a tool to provide you with information about your entrepreneurial profile, there are immediate clues to your future as a business owner in the responses you have given.

If you have indicated fifteen or more strong traits, there is a good possibility that you have been involved in your own business in the past or, at least, have worked in a managerial capacity for someone else. You have the positive personality traits required to be a successful business owner. If you have between eight and fifteen "S" responses, you are basically a positive and directed person and should not have any problem with improving certain areas to increase your personal business success potential.

If you have fewer than eight "S" responses, this is an indication that finding a complementary business partner who can support your goals may be an option worth considering. ■

Notes

Key Points

_____

_____

_____

_____

Personal Thoughts

_____

_____

_____

_____

_____

_____

Additional Research

_____

_____

_____

_____

_____

3

Profits in the Information Age

Overview of Newsletter Publishing

Americans like newsletters. We are a society of people who enjoy information. We like to get it briefly and clearly. We like it to look good, and we like to be able to carry it around with us as easily as possible. Is there a better form, during this, the information age, than a newsletter?

The surge of newsletter mania began around 1970. The first newsletter in North American was introduced in 1704. The

---

Overview of the Newsletter Publishing Business

This is a creative field which has excellent profit potential. Popularity of newsletters is predicted to continue at a steady rate. This business can easily be set-up as a home-based operation. Computers expand potential for growth.

'Shoestring' Start-up Investment:	$ 100
(Small classified ad)	
Average Start-up Investment:	$ 5,000
(Direct mail compaign)	
High Start-up Investment:	$ 25,000
(Direct mail compaign/computer)	
Break-even Point:	One to three years
Average Annual Gross Revenues:	$ 5,000 to $ 50,000
Potential Annual Gross Revenues:	$150,000 +

Boston News Letter reported ship arrivals and other commercial information people no longer learned efficiently by word of mouth. Editor John Campbell wrote articles, selected illustrations, composed type, supervised printing, and kept track of addresses. Versatility paid. It still does.

Since that time we have become more concerned with specialization, and finding more in-depth material about specific topics that interest us. Businesses have found an increasing need to keep up on business-related and/or industry-related information.

Part of this is the desire and the need to stay up-to-date on current developments, and part is a throw-back to the early days of personal journalism and intensive letter-writing among like-minded souls.

The Five Basic Steps of Newsletter Production

1. Gathering the information you will need for each issue.
2. Maintaining up-to-date files of source material from clippings, associations, specialists, and your readers.
3. Writing stories, headlines, and other copy for the issue.
4. Designing the format, including title and date, logo, and a "look." This also includes the layout, type styles, and graphics.
5. Duplicating the newsletter by photocopying, mimeography, or offset printing.

Broad Applications

Newsletters have become an every day necessity for corporations, associations, labor unions, and a variety of non-profit organizations as a means of quick communication. Some companies use them for internal communication among employees; others use them for external communication, including sales, and public and shareholder relations. Trade associations use the newsletter as a basic membership communications tool.

Public relations organizations find it useful to reach a specific audience, and delight in the fact that it is a "controlled" message—unlike a press release, which can be altered. Publicists are tickled with them because newsletters are generally receptive to publicist information; and no matter the size of circulation, the readership is generally intensive.

Many journalists are leaving their jobs with newspapers and magazines to enter the newsletter field. There is a demand for experts in subscription promotion and fulfillment. The Newsletter Association, an industry trade group, estimates that at least 11,000 different for-profit newsletters were published in the U.S. in 1986, twice the amount indicated five years before.

Steady Growth Predicted

The Newsletter Clearinghouse, a company that tracks newsletters, predicts a twelve to fifteen percent annual growth rate in newsletters over the next five years. There is good reason for this. So many people have a need for so much information on their jobs and in their lives, and they simply do not have the time to wade through, say, a 100-page report when an 8-page newsletter will give them the meat of the information they need.

If you think you have a super idea for a newsletter, think about the size of your audience and the price it will pay for your information. If the entire U.S. will buy your newsletter, you can make millions of dollars by charging a few cents a copy. If you can round up only 100 readers, each one must pay thousands of dollars before you can even dream about getting rich.

Production Guidelines

A one page newsletter printed on both sides of the paper will take between ten and fifteen hours to produce, from the news gathering stage to taking your camera-ready copy to the printer.

A four page newsletter printed on both sides will take approximately twenty-five hours.

These estimates do not take into consideration the unwritten law that things invariably take longer than predicted.

Easy to Start

It is not difficult to get started publishing a newsletter. But you must have the ability to write, type, and spell well. Many first-timers start out by typing up a one-page letter on a standard typewriter. They keep their day jobs and write the newsletter at night.

Some husband and wife teams start with one spouse holding down a full-time job while the other gets the newsletter started, making sure that there is at least one paycheck the couple can count on.

Professional-looking newsletters are best produced on a computer, although a typewriter will certainly do at first. If you do not type or spell very well, it is possible to hire freelance editors and typists to help you with the work. However, in the beginning stages it is best to keep personnel to a minimum—namely, just you—to keep costs down.

Qualifications

Most people who start newsletters are either journalists, publishers, or free-lance writers. However, if you have a wealth of information on a single subject that you think is valuable to a great number of people —that may be the only qualification you need.

You will require cash flow to pay for advertising, reproduction of the newsletter, and mailing expenses until the subscriptions start rolling in. You will want to receive and read as many newsletters as you can get your hands on. Some of them will offer you new ideas and often inspire you to come up with original ideas. Even though there may be other newsletters already in existence on the topic you feel you know best, there is always a market for a fresh approach to an old idea, so don't be afraid to give it a chance.

If, for example, you wanted to publish a newsletter on the music business, but you knew there were already several on the market, you would find a new angle, perhaps music for children, new music products, or music and computers, and gear your newsletter for a specialized market.

How Newsletters Get Started

There have always been many financial newsletters; but two women came up with an idea to publish a newsletter geared especially for women. *Moneypaper* was a down-to-earth financial newsletter designed to help women get the most out of the money they make. The co-founders of this newsletter started it in an attic workroom and have, by the way, a majority of male subscribers.

Sometimes newsletters begin out of a necessity or out of a common every-day occurrence that provides a person with a wealth of capsulated information on a certain subject matter. A lady named Dorothy Reines became an expert on nutrition and holistic medicine while nursing her husband through a long and demanding illness.

Her quarterly newsletter, *Healternatives,* gathered current trends and facts from various agencies involved in nutritional research. At the time she stopped publishing it, she had 10,000 subscribers across the U.S., and the income she earned covered all of her husband's medical expenses not covered by insurance.

Profit Potential

Annual gross revenues can range from pocket money to millions, depending on your marketing skills, the price, and demand for your newsletter. Pre-tax profits will also vary. Surprisingly, most newsletters show a loss while providing substantial cash flow. Spinoff products and services related to the subject matter can add quite a bit to profits.

As an example of this, the newsletter *Pethouse* was started by a young couple who are tremendously interested in animals. They were able to build up gross income to $10,000 their first year through a low-budget advertising and direct mail campaign. It wasn't until they started to promote pet products developed by entrepreneurs like themselves that they really started to realize a healthy profit. By the beginning of their third year, subscriptions were bringing in $15,000, but products were bumping their gross up to $40,000!

The Newsletter Clearinghouse publishes *Newsletter on Newsletters* and charges $84 per year for a semi-monthly perspective on the industry. If you are starting your own newsletter, you will more than likely be very interested to read such a publication. But will you pay $84 per year to get it? If you think the success of your newsletter is worth it, you will, and that is the secret of the industry!

Milton Zelman published his bimonthly *Chocolate News* on chocolate-scented paper. With 18,000 chocolate subscribers across the country paying $9.95, Zelman grossed about $180,000 a year very quickly. Most of this, he claims, was sheer profit as his overhead costs were quite low.

While still in his twenties, Mark Hulber invested $5,000 to launch a newsletter that evaluates the recommendations and monitors the predictions of other newsletters in the investment field. He has about 5,000 subscribers paying $135 — almost $350,000 in annual gross revenues.

Satisfying Your Subscribers

Newsletter publishers primarily rely on subscription rates for income, not on advertising, as newspapers and magazines do. Getting consumers to purchase your newsletter will be an easy task if your newsletter contains vital information — no frills, little or no advertising—just up-to-date inside information on what's happening in the field.

Many business people believe a newsletter pays for itself when it provides information they need to be competitive — to make decisions about whether to invest or cut back. They find out which markets are hot and which are not.

Some businesses actually decide that they can't afford not to subscribe if they think their competition is subscribing. Even with high rates, the newsletter subscription costs less than the time needed to put together all the information that is in the newsletter. So you see, newsletters can and do make money.

In determining what you will charge for your newsletter, you will want to figure out your overhead costs — typing, writing, photocopying, printing, mailing, etc. — and then figure in what you need to live on, plus of course, a profit. You must consider the amount of time it takes you to acquire and assemble the information you get, including the calls to your printer, picking up newsletters from the printer, and taking them to the mail service. The bottom line, however, is that the amount of money you make in the long run is determined by how many people you can get to subscribe. ■

4

Finding Your Audience

What's Your Subject?

Do you have a specialized knowledge in a given area? Are you a whiz on computers? Do you have real estate or health care expertise? If you choose a subject that you already know a lot about, you will have a head start. Perhaps you have a hobby shared by others who would appreciate new and different ideas. Or maybe you have done extensive research to deal with a particular problem, and there are thousands of potential readers who would like to benefit from your knowledge and experience.

What's Your Focus?

You do not want to cover too broad a subject. The narrower your focus, and the more detailed and specific you are, the more valuable your information becomes. People who want the kind of specific information you offer will gladly pay for the convenience of having it at their fingertips in one neat little package. Your newsletter often means a savings of time and money for these people.

What's the Competition?

Consult the *Oxbridge Directory of Newsletters* or the *National Directory of Investment Newsletters,* as well as the *Newsletter on*

Newsletters all available at many libraries, to determine whether or not your idea has been taken. Ideally, there is no other newsletter that would match yours. If there are others in existence, don't get discouraged. You will want to look at them to determine whether or not you have an angle that's unique and can be translated into a newsletter.

What is the Newsletter's Content?

Your information must be timely and authoritative. The content is more important than the layout, although you do want it to be pleasing to the eye. A greeting card newsletter might contain poems, sayings and witty remarks. Business people, however, are the ones willing to pay premium prices, and they want facts.

Newsletters are generally brief—between two and eight pages—with short pages wide margins for easy reading. The most common format is a two-column page. Writing style should be direct and to the point and the layout should be simple and consistent so that it is easily recognizable. Your most newsworthy material should be on the front page. A calendar of events is common and is a good draw. People will often subscribe just to find out about upcoming trade shows, seminars, meetings, and conventions.

How to Find Subscribers

If you have chosen your subject matter carefully, selling subscriptions will be merely a matter of reaching people in your target group. How do you do this?

1. Look through trade association directories, conference registers and other newsletters. Develop a mailing list and prepare material to send out to these qualified prospects.

2. Many organizations will actually provide lists of members if your newsletter contains information they find helpful.
3. "Direct Mail List Rates and Data" is a guide to mailing lists that you can rent or use as a research tool at the library. Your Yellow Pages will have a listing under "Direct Mail," "Mailing Lists" or "Advertising—Direct Mail." Rental rates are generally less than $100 per thousand names.
4. Place small ads in trade journals or special interest publications.

What Should You Charge?

We mentioned previously that your subscription price must cover printing and postage costs, as well as your time for research, writing, and promotion. After your costs are met, price becomes a matter of what the market will bear.

Some newsletters sell for as little as $5 per year; others, for as much as $1,000. Since your major expenses are printing and postage, you may find it more profitable to limit your circulation, i.e, go for a specialized audience, and charge a higher rate.

Expand into Publishing Business Directories

Why would a business owner choose to advertise in a local directory when such media as TV, radio, newspapers, and Yellow Pages reach so many people? Cost, of course! Advertising is expensive. Direct mail, though often very effective, is also expensive.

A business owner would have to spend $5,000 to reach 25,000 people. That's a lot of money. Word of mouth advertising is slow. Business directories are one answer. Low budget home businesses in particular get a lot of mileage out of business directories.

The evidence for the need for directories is conclusive. More and more people are choosing self-employment as a means to make a living. People in business for themselves are budget minded and are always be looking for inexpensive ways to reach their customers. Directories have become a very popular method of advertising.

Once you have established yourself with your newsletter, it is very easy to segue into directory publishing, which will not only increase your income but also automatically extend your newsletter market.

Getting Started

Directory publishing requires very little capital to get started and it holds a great deal of promise for being a money-making venture. As with any other business, it is important to analyze your market. Does your area of specialization have plenty of potential advertisers on a national or international level to support a directory? If not, are there supplemental areas you can include?

The ideal market base for a directory is between 35,000 and 100,000 names. Individuals and/or groups buy a listing in the directory. You can find advertisers by checking telephone books (available in major libraries) of large cities for associations within your industry or area of interest. Contact the organizations and explain the project, asking them if they would be willing to:

1. Give you access to their membership lists, or
2. Help you promote the directory through their own mailings and publications. You may be able to get more cooperation by offering to list their organization at no charge.

Important note: Before you begin to sell ad space, you must be certain that you will finish your directory. If you are not able to fulfill your commitment of producing the directory, you will have to refund all the money you have collected—a tiresome, frustrating, and depressing prospect. Therefore, it is wise to allot sixty percent of your ad revenues to cover printing costs.

Once the directory has been published, you will have provided a valuable resource for others involved in your area of interest and—the big bonus—will have access to one of the most comprehensive mailing lists available, to further promote your newsletter. ■

5

A Marketing Overview

Now that you have selected the kind of business you want to operate, it is important to explore the need for it. A process called *marketing research* will provide you with the information you need to develop your newsletter publishing business, plan methods of distribution or promotion, and set prices which are tailored to the audience you hope to attract.

In addition, your marketing research will provide you with information that will help when you are making decisions about a location, hours of operation, the specific types of services and/or products to sell, and how to gear your advertising.

Identifying Your Market

The process of identifying your audience may seem to be an extremely complex process, however, you can develop a perfectly workable and valuable marketing report by using the guidelines which follow and adapting them to your particular situation. Basically, there are five factors used to target the market:

Population. The number of households in the region you are considering as a target for your business is crucial as you must have a sufficient population base to produce the sales you need to generate a profit. Equally important is the circulation and age range of the readers of the magazines where you will be focusing your advertising for specific products. If, for example, you are planning to sell products for infants, a pub-

34

lication whose readership is largely of retirement age would be inappropriate. It would, however, work in your favor if you are promoting health products or even gift items.

Income. Your potential customers must have the income to purchase goods and services. Consumers in the 35-65 age group generally have considerable income which they spend on household items, personal grooming and sporting goods. This is not to discount the over-65 age group, a large and growing segment of the nation's population which, depending on the region, has adequate discretionary income (money after taxes and necessities) to spend, or the 18-35 age group, which is a desirable market for clothing, personal and recreational items.

Competition. The recent heavy promotion of "Tennis Bracelets" popularized by Chris Evert-Lloyd made it difficult for late-comers to make a dent in the market. This is almost always the case and, therefore, competition shouldn't be a negative factor. Rather, it should spur you on to stretch your creativity by coming up with something brand new or a similar product or service that is superior to those being offered by the competition—either in quality, selection, or price.

Product or service market match. Basically, this means that you must be able to attract those consumers whom you have the resources to serve. As an example, if your idea of the perfect business involves national distribution of your patented weight-training equipment, you must:

1. Reach an audience that is receptive and interested in body building through a carefully designed advertising campaign, and
2. Have the financing available to supply and ship the product.

Desire. Your objective is to match your product or service to the needs and desires of a particular group of consumers who will be responsive.

It is often difficult to figure out exactly what your target market wants. However, through observation of what the competition is doing, it should be possible to recognize a need.

Market Research Techniques

Large corporations often have in-house marketing staffs which conduct extensive research on a continuing basis to ensure that the products or services being offered are in line with the marketplace.

Obviously, this is an expensive and time-consuming process; one that you undoubtedly want to avoid.

Through several easy and inexpensive methods, you can find out everything you want to know about your potential market. The first step, however, is to determine exactly what information you need. It might be trends in population figures or regional economy, or how many people are active in a particular hobby.

The nearest Census Bureau office and your local Chamber of Commerce are consistently good sources for regional statistics. The reference librarian at the public library can steer you towards other local data and fact sheets which will give you the specifics you seek. In addition, the Small Business Administration compiles extensive marketing information, in addition to material on operating procedures for specific types of businesses.

Check the Directory of Trade Associations at the library to find the name and address of the advisory board for the mail order industry (or check the Resources listed at the end of this book). These trade boards exist to provide associates with marketing statistics, management tips and a wealth of valuable information. Often it only takes a phone call to get more details than you could ever use.

Another excellent source of information on population, income and sales figures is the annual survey of buying power published by *Sales and Marketing Management Magazine*, which breaks the information down by county and city in the United States.

Other Resources

The advertising departments of magazines and newspapers undoubtedly have Media Kits available for potential advertisers, which they will gladly send you upon request. These packets contain a breakdown of their advertising rates and specifications, a description of why advertising with them is to your benefit and, most important, a profile of their readership. A friendly conversation with one of their salespeople should give you a wealth of data.

Five Factors Used to Target your Market

1. Population
2. Income
3. Competition
4. Market Match
5. Desire

The people from whom you will be buying supplies, equipment, and products are another excellent source. They can give you a good run-down on trends, as well as an overview of current sales figures for their products. Since they are hoping you will eventually use them as a supplier for your business, they will be more than happy to give you free information.

It is, of course, often possible to gauge what the competition is doing and to wean information from them. There are two approaches when talking to people who are soon to be in direct competition. One is to be up-front and honest about your business plans and appeal to their sense of "industry spirit."

Surprisingly, you will find the direct approach works in the majority of cases as most people are genuinely interested in and supportive of others trying to make it in their field. It is better for everyone if "industry" standards are maintained and competitors have a healthy rapport. And, except in extreme situations such as a very small community, there is generally enough business to go around. It shouldn't be difficult to capture your share of the market, especially if you can develop something unique to attract it.

On the other hand, if competitors are less than receptive, it may be necessary to partake in a bit of super-sleuthing to get the information you want. A little brainstorming with friends should result in a few good ideas if you find it necessary to resort to investigative techniques.

The "Focus" Group

If you really want to go into depth with your marketing study, you might consider gathering together a group of people (family members, a social or church group, or friends) for a "focus" session to determine whether your product or service will match the needs of the prospective audience. This involves presenting your proposed business idea, with product samples if available, and creating a questionnaire that calls for specific answers from the group members.

This method is often used by major companies when they are testing new products and, in fact, there are private companies around the nation that do nothing but put focus groups together and set up testing sites in stores, shopping malls, and on street corners to obtain spontaneous and objective input from potential consumers.

The questions you would want to include on your questionnaire would ideally cover such aspects as how often members of the focus group have used a similar service or product in the past, what they liked about it, what they found to be unsatisfactory, how they feel it could have been improved, whether they would be willing to try another, their age, income, and any specifics that relate to your proposed business.

Analyzing Your Marketing Research

The bottom line in conducting your research is that you want to zero in on information which provides insights on the potential for your business idea before you invest time, money and energy in setting it up.

If, for example, you were considering starting your mail order company with a fishing lure guaranteed to work and your research indicated that ninety percent of the millions of fishermen in America prefer to use worms, you would definitely want to reconsider the validity of your concept. On the other hand, if your marketing research pointed out that sixty percent of the fishermen are always on the lookout for a new lure, the potential for your product would be much greater and advertising it in appropriate magazines would probably guarantee a profitable venture.

Buy an inexpensive notebook to help you keep track of your marketing data. Use a separate page for each category you are researching. The notebook will serve as your personal, on-going market study to be reviewed and amended as your business grows and the audience you are serving changes.

The greatest thing in the world is not so much where we stand as in what direction we are moving.

Oliver Wendell Holmes

Plan to update information pages as new studies are published (generally an annual event) indicating changes in population, economy or buying and spending trends. Most newspapers publish synopses of local, state and federal studies of this nature, so maintaining your notebook shouldn't be a problem. You should also reserve several pages to record comments and suggestions from customers once your business is established, which will help you personalize your business to the market and will keep you a step ahead of the competition.

Spend as much time as you need to feel comfortable about your marketing project. For some people this might mean two hours at the City Clerk's office, while others may want to devote a week or more to gathering and analyzing information to incorporate into their business plan.

The important point is that the results of your research are comprehensive enough to provide you with concrete information on who your potential customers are and how you can best reach them. ■

Review

- I have completed my entrepreneurial profile to determine my strengths and weaknesses. _____
- My friends and/or relatives have given me additional input based on the profile. _____
- I am aware of the advantages and disadvantages of going into business for myself. _____
- I have prepared and reviewed my Business Capabilities Application. _____
- Time is not a problem; I can easily devote the time I'll need to build my business. _____
- The important people in my life are supportive of my decision. _____
- I have analyzed my personal cash flow to ensure that I can support myself and my family for at least six months or until the business is solvent. _____
- I feel confident about my future as a business owner at this point. _____
- I know what people want as far as my business is concerned. _____
- I have conducted informal studies to determine my potential customers and understand their needs. _____
- I have analyzed the competition, know what they offer, and have a general idea about their success ratio. _____
- I have done my marketing research and know how to get in touch with the audience I want to reach. _____
- I have contacted the trade association for my industry and have accumulated facts and figures regarding the pros and cons of starting my own business. _____
- I feel confident that my product or service is salable. _____

6

Location: Commercial vs. Home-Based

The majority of newsletter publishers we spoke with operate out of their home. Since they never see their clients, they usually rent a post office box, install a second line on the telephone, and function quite effectively. There were a few, however, who publish more than one title and, primarily because of information gathering and maintenance, opt to rent a small office.

Space requirements for a newsletter publishing business, whether at home or in an office, are relatively minimal. The equipment your need to operate efficiently takes up very little room—everything, even a light box for ease in pasteup and a computer (which allows you to do pasteup directly on the screen), can fit on a large desk—and the rest depends on how much elbow room and storage space you need. For the home-based business, anything from a corner of the kitchen to a spare bedroom will suffice.

"Clean" Industry

A good size bookcase and a few filing cabinets or stacking shelves should be more than enough space for storage and reference materials. (One of the nice things about newsletter publishing is that it is essentially "clean," and unless you're in the habit of leaving papers all over the place, your workspace can stay tidy and organized.)

If you decide to use a computer to produce your newsletters, an important consideration in setting up working space is electrical cords and cables. With one machine, you won't need to worry too much about tripping over wires. If you have a printer and maybe a copier, however, you will have wires running from here to there and back as part of your work area, which is both unattractive and a hazard. In planning your space, consult with a local computer store about ideal configurations.

General Guidelines for Commercial Locations

Selecting the right location is vital to the success of your business. The first factors you must analyze when looking for a commercial location are:

1. The community you want to live and/or work in, based on family needs, finances, your preference for a particular area because of health reasons or the fact that you have an established reputation in a certain area, and
2. The locations available within that community.

These factors are interrelated. On one hand, you may want to settle down in an area with a limited number of suitable business locations available. But on the other hand, you may have run across a number of potentially viable sites in several communities or areas, in which case an investigation of each must be conducted, covering each of the points listed below:

1. *The type of business you are planning to operate.* Retail, wholesale and service businesses have slightly different requirements as determined by the type of products or service being offered and the market potential in a specific area.
2. *The demographics of the area.* This includes the number of consumers who want or need your product or service and are willing and able to pay your price; the median income and employment opportunties; age ranges of the major

population group; the volume of retail trade and projected expansion data, available from census reports and Chamber of Commerce business reports accumulated during your market research project.

3. *Competition.* You must determine how many similar establishments are serving the market and how successful their business is to decide if there is room for your new venture. The best way to do this is by compiling from the phone book a list of businesses that you feel will be direct competition and visiting their locations at different times of day to observe the activity levels and to talk with employees, who should be willing to answer your questions if you approach them in a friendly way, i.e., "The store is really quiet right now. Is it always so slow at this time of day?" Often, the same kind of research can be accomplished effectively on the telephone.

4. *Traffic patterns.* Is your proposed location close to freeways, major intersections and/or a central business district? Is there sufficient parking? Is the foot traffic past the location strong and steady enough to guarantee walk-in trade, if needed, to generate sales and profits? The ease with which customers can get to your store is a major consideration in terms of success.

5. *Your image.* Decide on the image you want to project, such as top-quality products, ultra-modern decor, superior service, low prices, or convenience, *before* you go scouting for locations.

6. *The product or service.* If you are planning to sell high-priced, state-of-the-art European electronic equipment, it would be advisable to locate your business in a mall or on the main street of an economically comfortable community to ensure getting the response you need to survive. Generally, there are specific areas within a marketplace that cater to consumers in specific income levels and/or occupational groups, i.e., executives, blue collar workers, stu-

dents, etc. Consider your product/service and the projected number of potential buyers within the community.

7. *The amount of rent required.* Locations having the highest potential of profit through consumer traffic (such as a prime downtown spot or shopping mall, a corner shop or a store with good frontage) are more expensive because competition keeps rents up to the maximum. The trade-off, however, is an increase in sales and, generally, a lower advertising budget because of the visibility factor.

As a new business owner, you may find that your allotted capital for rent is limited. Therefore, understanding and exploring the factors involved in selecting a location will help you find the best one for your money.

Retail Locations

The guidelines indicated above are applicable for retail businesses. Poor location is one of the chief causes of failure among retail stores, and, on the other hand, the right location can be all it takes for even a mediocre business to thrive and grow.

Service Businesses

When clients are going to be visiting your place of business, the same principles of location selection apply as are indicated for retail. If, however, clients will not be visiting, location selection can be based on rent, the amount of space needed and the convenience to you.

Wholesale or Manufacturing Businesses

Where you locate a wholesale business depends on your market. If dealing primarily with local retailers or customers, your location should be within easy driving distance of your clientele.

However, if most of your business is conducted through the mails or delivery services, you can base your selection on the best rent available and the convenience factor for you and your staff. When choosing a location for your wholesale business, warehousing needs are a vital consideration, as is projected expansion.

Before You Sign a Lease

In all but the most unusual cases, such as renting your location from a family member or accepting a temporary agreement in a building that is for sale, you will be required to sign a lease before moving into your new location. The most desirable agreement for you as a new business owner is a one- to two-year lease with a renewal option and a guaranteed rate of rent increases over a five- to ten-year period.

Rent for a commercial location is established either on a flat rate or a percentage basis. Under the flat rate, rent is generally based on the square footage of the shop, and on the location, or in some cases, on potential volume. The percentage basis involves a base amount of rent plus a prearranged percentage of monthly sales.

Your lease will also cover a number of other points, such as the liabilities and responsibilities of the landlord and of you, the tenant, i.e., who is to pay for specific repairs, renovations, tax increases, and utilities, etc.

The lease may contain stipulations about the size of the exterior sign you can erect, hours of operation, insurance coverage, and assignation of the lease to another party (a sublet).

Before signing a lease to set up your business, make sure that gas, electrical, and water lines are adequate enough to handle high volume usage, that you have restrooms and changing areas for employees, and convenient parking and loading areas. Also check with the leasing agent to be certain you can make leasehold improvements, i.e., storage shelves, at your discretion as the business warrants it.

It is recommended that you have an attorney review the lease carefully before you sign it to ensure you understand all of the clauses and to serve as a negotiator, if necessary.

Setting up Your Business at Home

Short of disrupting family patterns on days when you are preparing items for shipping, there is a lot of appeal in operating your mail order business out of your own home.

Thousands of successful businesses have been started in a basement, a spare room or on the kitchen table. Henry Ford, for example, founded the Ford Motor Company in his garage and Jean Nidetch started Weight Watchers in her living room as a support group for friends who wanted to lose extra pounds. Both of these businesses, and many more like them, became successful full-fledged corporations, despite humble beginnings.

The Small Business Administration estimates that there are close to ten million home-based businesses in the United States today and, of these, more than thirty percent are owned and operated by women. These figures have been substantiated by an AT&T study, as well as by the U.S. Department of Labor.

Starting a home-based business has provided an opportunity for many people who might otherwise never have the chance to become entrepreneurs.

For others, a home-based business is the ticket out of the world of the urban commuter. In fact, a home-based business is the perfect way to try something new to see how it works while still working another job to pay the bills. Once the business has proven itself and is realizing a profit, you can leave the job to devote full time to your new venture.

Couples often find that investing time and energy in building a business together at home develops stronger relationships in addition to increasing joint income. For the retired and for those with physical disabilities, it is a path to staying involved, exploring self-sufficiency and guaranteeing a profitable future.

Start-Up Steps Never Change

As with any new business whether located at home or in a commercial location, it is important to follow the basic guidelines for start-up, including conducting a market survey, drawing up a business plan, setting goals, reviewing capital needs and projected income, developing an advertising campaign, and establishing a professional image.

The Advantages of Establishing a Home-Based Business

- Ability to start your business immediately
- Minimal start-up capital needed
- No rent or excessive set-up charges for utilities required
- Comfortable working conditions
- Reduced wardrobe expenses
- No commuting
- Tax benefits
- Elimination of office politics
- Flexibility and independence
- Full utilization and recognition of skills
- Low risk for trial and error

Many businesses, especially in the areas of service and mail order, can easily be set up in the home, offering a number of advantages for the beginning business owner.

Setting up your business at home automatically eliminates up to seventy-five percent of the start-up costs and responsibilities required for an office or storefront operation. You are, in your home, already making rent or mortgage payments and paying for telephone service, insurance, and utilities.

At bare minimum, a commercial location will require $10,000 just to open the doors with basic merchandise and/or equipment. In addition, valuable time and energy is saved because you don't have to scout for the location, have utilities installed, or decorate the premises.

Getting Your Feet Wet

A home-based business gives you the opportunity to test the waters with a minimum of risk. This is especially beneficial to first-time entrepreneurs, who may prefer to learn and grow with the business in the comfort of home without the pressures that operating out of a commercial location often bring.

As a hedge against inflation, the home-based business is a natural. In addition to low start-up, tax deductions for use of home as office provide relief from a seemingly endless outflow of cash for mortgage or rent payments. You must, however, be aware of the tax laws, which allow deductions only for that part of the home "used exclusively and regularly" for business and, as of last year, limited to a modified net income of the business.

After the business is running smoothly, you will find that the potential to earn money is greater because of reduced overhead. Your production will increase because you have more control over your schedule and fewer of the typical interruptions that arise in a commercial setting. Generally, home-based entrepreneurs claim that an added benefit is reduced stress, despite the fact that they are working long hours.

Of course, as with any business arrangement, there are also disadvantages to setting up your business in your home. By recognizing them, however, it is possible to address and minimize the problems before they come up.

Getting to Work

One of the biggest problems faced by home-based entrepreneurs is being able to establish a productive work schedule. There are different types of interruptions that come up in a home environment, including visits from friends and neighbors, household chores that need to be done, the temptation of television and the daily paper when there is work to be produced, and the fact that there is no one around to spur you on.

A helpful suggestion for getting down to work is to dress in the morning as if you were going out to a regular job. This alone will help you set your priorities for the day.

The best solution, however, is to establish regular working hours from the onset (although you do have the flexibility as a home-based business owner to arrange your schedule around the times you know you are the most productive).

If friends want to visit, politely explain to them that you are operating a business which requires your full concentration and arrange a suitable time to get together according to your schedule.

It is also important, if you have family, that they are supportive and willing to arrange their lives as much as possible around your schedule. This can be dealt with through frequent family discussions about what you are doing and how the business operates.

Another difficult area is learning to separate business and pleasure. A home-based business often makes it very easy to work day and night on a project. Again, it is important to allot time for personal activities. The secret to remember is that the work will get done much more efficiently if you are relaxed and rested.

It is also a good idea, if at all possible, to have the business set up in a separate room or area that can be closed off from your personal living space after working hours. In this way, you will be less inclined to take care of some little business detail just because you happen to see it staring you in the face from the kitchen table.

The Disadvantages of a Home-Based Business

- Success is based 100% on your efforts
- Difficulty in establishing solid work habits
- Difficult to know how to set competitive rates
- Limited support system
- Isolation
- Limited work space
- Disruption of personal life
- Clients are uncomfortable coming to your home
- Zoning restrictions

Home-based business owners often experience feelings of isolation from those in their industry. One way to eliminate this is to join local groups, such as the Chamber of Commerce and networking groups, and at least, to attend the meetings.

Check to see how many members are entrepreneurs, which will give you a built-in support system. By making yourself available to serve on committees, you will also be able to reach further into the community and publicize your business for the cost of your involvement.

Review Your Local Laws

Before getting started, it is important to check that zoning ordinances in your area will allow you to use your home for business purposes. Since zoning ordinances vary from city to city and county to county, it is necessary to contact the Planning Department of your regional government offices or talk with your attorney to find out what is allowed, based on the type of business, the area to be used within your home, noise control, tax regulations, business signs and other aspects, as well as if you need a special permit or license to operate.

If you are expecting clients to visit your home for business, it is best to have a separate room set up as an office so that when they do come to discuss a job, they won't feel as if they are intruding on a family. If, however, an office is out of the question, make sure you arrange meetings during times when the family is away from home to ensure that there will be no interruptions.

God gives every bird its food,
but he does not throw it in the nest.

J. G. Holland

Another option is to go to the client's location when you must have meetings or offer pick-up and delivery service, if applicable. Depending on the business, however, and the quality of your work, client discomfort shouldn't be a major problem, according to a number of home-based business owners we have interviewed.

As an example, the number of home-based typesetting services has increased dramatically over the past few years and we have never heard of any complaints or problems in this area. The bottom line, as far as the customer is concerned, is still—and will always be—reliable service or high quality products and the knowledge that they are dealing with a professional.

If your business is suited to being home-based, it is an option that warrants exploration. The benefits to the beginning entrepreneur can mean the difference between working for someone else and turning a dream into reality.

The key elements, as with any business, are motivation, a needed product or service, careful planning and the desire to succeed. Sometimes just knowing that the expenses of establishing a business in a commercial location are alleviated by setting up a home-based enterprise is enough to push you forward to success, one small step after another. ■

Review

If setting up my business at home, I have:

- Checked with the City and County offices in my area regarding required licenses and permits and zoning regulations for home-as-office. _____
- Set aside a room or an area in my home that will be used exclusively for my business. _____
- Had a separate telephone installed and have purchased an answering machine or contracted with a message service. _____
- Set up a separate business bank account. _____
- Informed friends and family of my business routine and specific working hours to reduce interruptions and distractions. _____

If setting up in a commercial location, I have:

- Investigated rental rates for the area I am interested in. _____
- Checked traffic flow, parking and foot-traffic around my proposed location. _____
- Determined that my business is compatible with others in the area. _____
- Talked with my prospective landlord about improvements, maintenance and rent increases. _____
- Had my lawyer check the rental agreement and any local zoning regulations. _____
- Secured the necessary operating licenses and permits from the City and/or County. _____

7

Figuring Costs and Filling in Charts

Having decided that you are ready and able to accept the challenge of starting your own business, it is necessary to take a look at your overall financial picture. Even if you have a healthy savings account, or feel you can start your business with a minimal capital investment, diagnosing your personal financial situation will help you determine ongoing expenses.

The easiest way to estimate how much money you will need to get your business started and to cover expenses, including personal living expenses for the first six months, is to prepare a *Cost of Living* or *Cash Flow Statement* and a *Projected Expense Chart*. Samples are provided on the following pages for your use.

Preparing the *Projected Expense Chart* will give you a fairly accurate picture of what it will cost to open the doors and indicate how much income you must generate to realize a profit. The other advantage of creating these charts early in the game is that when you find that you want to explore funding options, you will already have two of the required documents prepared and will only need to update them.

The first step in examining your financial situation is to ask yourself the following questions:

1. Do I generally pay my bills on time or wait until my creditors start sending me collection notices?
2. Have I regularly reconciled my bank statement so I know how much money I have in my checking account at any given time?

3. Is my philosophy "If I've got it, I spend it," or do I typically carefully plan how I am going to use my income?
4. Have I ever developed a personal budget so I know how much money is coming in, how much is going out and what I have left over?

These are important aspects of your financial personality that will be helpful to understand when running your business. As your business and subsequent involvement with financial matters grows, it will be vital that you have a handle on your philosophy about money. And there is no time like the beginning, when your business concept is being formed, to start learning.

The Cash Flow Statement

Using the chart on Page 58, you can determine your personal living expenses for the past three to six months, to help you gauge what you will need to survive during the early stages of your business.

The easiest way to complete the statement is to use your checkbook register (if you write checks for most purchases), and/or cash receipts and copies of money orders as research tools. If your expenses are relatively consistent from month to month, you should be able to get an overview by analyzing one month. A more accurate picture will emerge if you break down income and expense for three to six months to account for periodic payments, such as taxes, insurance and seasonal spending.

Using the samples provided, fill in the amounts in each category from your checkbook register or receipts. Use a separate sheet for every month that you are analyzing. For miscellaneous spending, a standard calculation is five percent of monthly income. Add up each month's expenses, total them all and then divide that figure by the number of months you are analyzing. This will give you an average monthly expense figure.

Follow the same procedure for income. You can then subtract your expenses from your income to see where you stand. If you have computed your figures accurately, you might run across a few surprises. It isn't unusual to discover that we spend more money than we realize, often on miscellaneous, unneeded purchases. You may be able to see some areas where you can cut back.

The main point, however, is that you now know:

1. How much of your own money, if any, you can afford to invest in your new business, and
2. What it costs you to live comfortably, which will help you set income goals for the business.

Start-Up Costs

Every business owner has specific standards about how they want to run their operation. One person may feel perfectly comfortable waiting until they are making a profit to order business cards. Another wouldn't dream of opening the doors without cards, brochures, and letterhead already printed.

You will have your own ideas about what you need before opening your business. Then, you must find out what it will cost and, if at all possible, prepare the *Start-Up Statement* as indicated in this chapter.

It is also advisable to figure how much it will cost to run the business for three to six months, using the sample *Projected Expense Forecast* which follows. A six-month projection should give you the opportunity to start getting an idea of what your profits will be down the line.

Cash Flow Statement
Month Of _____

Income		Expenses	
Wages	$_____	Rent or mortgage	$_____
Miscellaneous	_____	Auto loan	_____
		Gas & car repairs	_____
TOTAL	$_____	Auto insurance	_____
		Life insurance	_____
		Medical insurance	_____
Savings	_____	Homeowners insurance	_____
		Taxes	_____
		Loan payments	_____
Credit Line	_____	Food: at home	_____
		Food: dining out	_____
		Telephone	_____
Home Equity	_____	Utilities	_____
		Household repairs, etc.	_____
		Medical bills	_____
		Credit card payments	_____
		Interest expense	_____
		Clothing/dry cleaning	_____
		Travel	_____
		Miscellaneous	_____
		Savings	_____
		TOTAL	$_____

Start-Up Costs

Furniture: Purchase price $_____

               Down payment required $_____

Fixtures: Purchase price   _____

               Down payment required   _____

Equipment: Purchase price   _____

               Down payment required   _____

Installation and delivery costs   _____

Decorating & leasehold improvements   _____

Deposits: utilities and rent   _____

Fees: legal, accounting, consulting, etc.   _____

Licenses & permits   _____

Starting inventory   _____

Supplies   _____

Printing   _____

Pre-opening advertising & promotion   _____

Miscellaneous   _____

            TOTAL start-up expense $_____

            Less available start-up capital $_____

            TOTAL amount needed $_____

Projected Expense Statement

Months:	1st	2nd	3rd	4th	5th	6th
Rent						
Utilities						
Telephone						
Insurance						
Professional services						
Taxes & licenses						
Advertising						
Office supplies						
Office equipment						
Inventory						
Business auto expense						
Travel expense						
Entertainment						
Dues & subscriptions						
Salaries						
Owner's draw						
Loan payments						
Interest payments						
Miscellaneous						
TOTAL						

Have this chart enlarged at your local copy shop if you are planning to use it as part of your Business Plan (see Chapter 12). Enlarging it will cost you a few cents, but using it will save you many dollars in the long run because of your increased awareness of your financial picture.

Preparing the *Start-Up Statement* and *Projected Expense Forecast* involves conducting some research. For example, to estimate the cost of business cards or letterhead stationery, contact several printers or copy shops in your area and obtain quotes. Call the local newspaper for prices on different types of ads, including display and classified.

An insurance agent will be able to give you an estimate on liability coverage. Check with the telephone company for information and rates on installing a phone line. You can also start to shop around to find the best prices on office supplies, equipment and materials you need to conduct business.

After you have completed your research, incorporate the information into the charts. Obviously, some of your figures, such as those for telephone expense and taxes, will be "guesstimated."

However, the final figure will give you a good idea of how much it is going to cost to get your business up and running for at least six months.

Utilizing the same theory, you can develop a *Projected Income Statement*, drawing from industry figures available through your trade association. This would include all income realized from cash sales, collection of outstanding invoices, credit card sales and miscellaneous income. By subtracting your total expenses from total income, you will get a clear picture of projected profit or loss.

All of these statements will be requested by loan officers, venture capitalists and the Small Business Administration (SBA) if and when you apply for a loan. They require this kind of paperwork to ensure that you have basic business knowledge, a commendable track record, and that you are serious about your venture.

You will also be required to fill out a personal financial statement (available through the lending institution), especially if you are the sole owner or a general partner in the business.

Your First Year Investment

Growth costs money. Although some entrepreneurs have started a newsletter for less than $10,000—the cost of a 5,000-piece direct mail campaign—the ideal capital investment is around $65,000, which includes $20,000 for a year's salary for you; $500 for an artist to design a special format for you; $8,000 to print the newsletter and direct mail solicitation pieces; $3,000 for postage; and $28,000 to rent mailing lists with the names of 80,000 people.

The rest of your money will go for telephone costs, lawyer's fees if you are incorporating, and other incidentals of day-to-day business. Your greatest expenditure is lining up subscriptions.

Tip #1
*Develop a format that is easy for you
to work with and that fits the
image you want the newsletter to project.*

An industry rule of thumb is that you should expect to spend $1 to attract $1 in subscription fees. So, if you charge $100 for your newsletter, it is likely that at least $100 will be spent on a direct mail campaign to bring in that subscription. A startup newsletter publisher will often send out 25,000 or more solicitations. A one percent to two and a half percent rate of response is considered average; three to five percent is incredible!

In your second year, when it's time to ask for renewals of subscriptions, you can expect two out of four subscribers to sign up again, providing you have fulfilled your editorial promise. Instead of $1, however, you may spend as little as 5 cents for every $1 worth of second-year subscriptions. At this point, you are grossing (before expenses and taxes) 95 cents out of very dollar sent in by a subscriber. While you will certainly spend some of that money on overhead and on searching out new subscriptions, a large portion is pure profit.

Keep The Search Going

You never want to stop prospecting for new subscribers. Lists of potential subscribers can be purchased from brokers and trade associations for between $40 to $100 per one thousand names. You can advertise in publications that appeal to your target audience as well as running a continual classified ad in general interest magazines.

Leave free copies of your newsletter (with an order form included, of course) in large hotels and tourist areas, hand them out at seminars and business meetings, offer them to groups and organizations that are involved in your area of specialization—distribute them any place you can think of that might have potential clients passing through. You may also consider selling your own list of subscribers to other publishers, making certain, of course, that they are not in direct competition with you!

It is possible that if you decide one day to quit publishing, there will be another publisher ready to buy your business because of the value of your readers' list of names and addresses. ■

8

Equipment and Supplies

Here's where things get both interesting and a little confusing. It certainly is possible to produce a newsletter on an old manual typewriter that you resurrected from the back of the closet. However, newsletter subscribers have become more sophisticated in these days of electronic publishing and expect professional material. This means either using an electric typewriter with a good clean ribbon cartridge to ensure clarity, or computer word processing.

A good electric typewriter will run anywhere from $200 used to $1,200 for the new electronic typewriters with memory storage. Buying a personal computer system can run from a minimum of $1,000 for a used one to $5,000 for a new top-of-the-line computer and the programs you need to operate it. A printer will cost between $1,000 for dot matrix capability to $5,000 for a high quality laser printer.

There are many different brands and models of computers on the market, so it is necessary to do some investigating before you buy. It is recommended, however, that you purchase one of the mainstream computer systems because of the availability of word processing software, the ability to expand your system as necessary for future growth, and the relative ease of finding parts and service.

For example, the Macintosh is considered to be the best computer for producing text and graphics, although IBM and its clones are catching up fast. In addition to being extremely simple to operate—"user friendly"—the Macintosh screen display approximates the type styles and sizes, and copy configurations you have designated so you can see how it will look when printed. A full page monitor has become a virtual necessity. The Macintosh SE or Macintosh II in conjunction with a LaserWriter Plus is considered to be the top of the line for electronic publishing capabilities.

There are many other models, such as the Tandy (Radio Shack) 2000, Compaq, Kaypro and dozens more which are less expensive and suitable for newsletter publishing. The biggest limitation, however, is with printing—many non-mainstream brands are not compatible with laser printers—so if high resolution is not an important factor, one of the less expensive brands may work fine.

Looking for Bargains

There are many ways to save money buying computer equipment and supplies, generally through third-party vendors and mail order sources. Apple and IBM equipment is sold only through authorized dealers, while IBM clones and non-Apple-produced Macintosh peripherals are available everywhere, from small stores to mail order businesses run by electronics whizzes who make their own computers and accessories.

The market is a smorgasbord. (A word of caution here: You need reliable equipment that is backed up by warranty. Whatever your decision on brand, make sure you are protected with a company that stands behind what it sells.)

Shopping around is the only way to get your best deal on equipment and software. If you live in a small town, buy a paper for the nearest big city and look for computer ads. You'll generally find your best deals advertised in the paper.

Values in Additional Supplies

As for peripherals and supplies, you will need a good source for such things as floppy disks, computer paper, software and so on. here are some mail order sources you can request catalogs from:

> **ComputerWare** (Macintosh)
> 490 California Ave.
> Palo Alto, CA 94306
> (415) 323-7559

> **MacWarehouse** (Macintosh)
> 1690 Oak Street
> PO Box 1579
> Lakewood, NJ 08701-1579
> (800) 255-6227

> **The Laser Connection** (Macintosh & PC)
> (800) 523-2696

> **Quill** (Office and computer supplies)
> 100 S. Schelter Rd.
> PO Box 4700
> Lincolnshire, IL 60197-4700

Your supply costs will depend on your equipment. Floppy disks for PCs are slightly less than Macintosh disks, for example. You should never want for suppliers, though. The computer industry is full of publications, organizations, and other resources from which you can learn of good, economical supply sources. Some of these resources are listed at the back of this book.

Checklist for Computer Shopping

• Will the computer handle the software programs you need?

- How much "K" does the software require?
- What will it cost to expand the system, if necessary?
- How many disk drives are needed to operate the system?
- How much set-up space is required for the computer, printer and peripheral equipment?
- Is the computer "user friendly" with easy-to-use commands and a comprehensive instruction manual?
- Does the software include a manual and/or a guided tour?
- What assistance does the software manufacturer provide—telephone information line, user newsletter or magazine, operating guarantees?
- How big is the monitor?
- What does the basic system price include (disk drive, keyboard, software)?
- What does the warranty cover and for how long?
- What kind of service contract is available? What will it cost?
- Does the dealer offer on-going support?
- Will the dealer provide training and assistance in working with the software or the system? Is this service free?
- What is the quality of the copy generated by the printer?
- How fast and how loud is the printer?
- Are other printers (i.e., Laser Writer, Laser Jet or Linotronic) compatible with the system?
- What is the total price of the system, peripherals and software?
- Is the dealer willing to put a quote in writing for comparison shopping?
- Is financing available? At what interest rate?

Other Equipment Needs

Equipment needs for your newsletter publishing business, in fact, are little more than that needed by the standard office-based business. Here is a general list of items you should have on hand to start the business:

1. *A telephone.* It sounds obvious, but most of your newsgathering and advertising placement will be done on a national basis. So make sure you have a reliable system, and investigate low-cost long-distance carriers.

2. *A file cabinet.* You can find these at second-hand stores. You can make use of either letter or legal size; try to get four drawers.

3. *A postal meter.* Using a meter will speed up your mailing.

4. *A storage shelf.* Also for storage of envelopes, promotional materials, and so on. You can find a wide selection of shelving at such places as Builder's Emporium, or any large home-improvement store.

5. *Furniture.* You are going to be spending the majority of your time sitting in front of your computer. Therefore, it is extremely important that you invest in the right desk and chair. Not only will the wrong furniture give you back and neck aches, studies have proven that it can cause extreme fatigue and a decrease in overall productivity.

   Your computer keyboard desktop should be no more than 26-inches from the ground. Even more important is the chair. It should provide support for the base of the spine, a backrest no higher than your shoulder blades and a seat that can be raised or lowered easily. A solid seat and rounded cushion to prevent the restriction of blood flow in the legs is recommended. And do yourself a favor: Buy a good desk lamp that will keep eyestrain to a minimum! Setting up your computer or typewriter near a window will provide good natural light to augment artificial lighting as well as giving you a welcome view while you are working.

6. *A postal scale.* Get a new one at the local office supply store. Using the postal scale will help you keep postage costs down.

7. *Card files.* This will help you track inquiries and orders, and help build a mailing list. A 3 x 5-inch index-card box will do the job.

8. *A book case.* You might find yourself building a small library of reference materials, as well as holding on to various trade publications. An inexpensive bookcase is a good way to keep everything in one place.

9. *Adding machine or calculator.* These aren't expensive, especially the small, battery-operated LED kind, and they'll make your life a lot easier. Find one with at least four functions and an eight-figure display.

10. *Typewriter.* Ask yourself how much you trust modern technology. If you've ever suffered a computer breakdown, you know the value of having a good typewriter on hand.

Stocking the Office

In addition to any equipment purchases you may decide to make, there's a range of office supplies you'll go through regularly. Find a local office supply store, or a mail-order office supplier (prices are often much better) to keep yourself in supply of:

- stapler and staples
- staple remover
- pencils and sharpener
- special non-reproducing pencils for copy
- erasers
- ball point pens
- calendars (wipe-on/off are great for publishing)
- paper clips
- 3x5-inch index cards
- address labels, self-adhesive or gummed
- manila folders, letter or legal size
- file folder labels
- cellophane tape
- stamp moistener
- rubber fingertips
- rubber cement

- white glue, wax, and rubber cement for pasteup
- X-acto knife and blades (No. 11 is best)
- rubber bands
- notepads and layout sheets
- letter opener
- typewriter supplies
- typing correction fluid
- computer supplies

Here are two mail-order office supply companies you can request catalogs from:

Colwell Systems, Inc.
201 Kenyon Rd.
P.O. Box 4025
Champaign, IL 61820–1325
(for business forms and stationery)

General Wholesale Products
2957 E. 46th St.
Los Angeles, CA 90058
(for office equipment, etc.)

The Financial Choice

You can buy new or used equipment from dealers and independent sellers. Or, if you don't mind rummaging through other people's lives, you can find incredible bargains on supplies and equipment at garage sales, swap meets, thrift shops run by charitable organizations, or auctions. Often, it is well worth the time involved because the savings can be tremendous.

Before investing money, do your homework. Talk with other business owners to find out which brand of equipment they use and why they prefer it over other choices on the market. This will help you make the best decision based on your needs and budget.

Also, talk with independent dealers who carry a broad line of similar types of equipment. They can give you insights on maintenance, longevity, service contracts, and prices.

They will also be able to tell you when to expect a drop in price for the item you are interested in, although you can count on seeing sales on major equipment such as computers or other major items, for example, during the first few months of the year, when manufacturers introduce their new models.

Cash or Credit?

Unless you are planning to pay cash for an equipment purchase, you will either make a down payment and set up a payment schedule with the dealer, or take out a loan with the bank. With interest rates for bank loans currently running at about fourteen percent you might be able to find a dealer who is willing to handle the financing at a lower rate.

Although this method is a less effective way of establishing creditworthiness, it will serve to get the business going. Another advantage is that if you should find youself in a tight cashflow situation at any time, a private dealer/lender with whom you have a personal relationship is much more likely to be flexible ... without charging you a penalty for late payment.

Buying Used Equipment

When buying used equipment from a dealer, the chances of it being in working condition are generally pretty good. Dealers have a reputation to uphold and will stand behind their merchandise, especially if they are firmly established in the community. There are, however, several ways you can scout around to ensure that the one you decide to work with is reputable:

- Find a store with membership in the local Chamber of Commerce. Although this is not an iron-clad guarantee, it does indicate the store ownership's interest in following business standards established within the community.
- If the dealer also sells new equipment, it is highly likely that much of the used equipment has been traded in by people who are upgrading. You may be able to get an excellent bargain on an item which has been well maintained by the former owner.
- If there is a service department on the premises, you can be assured that used equipment has been reconditioned before being put on sale. It also increases your chances of getting fast, inexpensive and reliable service if needed at a later date.
- Used equipment dealers realize that it is not always easy to find a buyer and should be willing to work with you. Shopping around will give you an idea of average prices and will give you the information you need to negotiate. If the dealer won't work with you, keep looking.
- What are the terms of the warranty? Even used equipment should be covered for a short time for parts and labor, especially if it has been overhauled or reconditioned.
- Is the dealer willing to agree to offer a trade-in allowance on the item you are buying when you decide to upgrade? Of course, there will be stipulations based on wear and tear and time, however he or she should be willing to consider it.

Buyer Beware

There are other ways to find and buy used equipment, but it falls into the realm of "Buyer Beware." If you choose to deal with private parties through the classified ads or with auctioneers selling off the inventory of a bankrupt business, you must be willing to take a chance. Although the prices will be easy on your budget, the cost of repairing a malfunctioning machine could result in a long-term drain on your profits.

The greatest inspiration is a
challenge to attempt the impossible.

A. Michelson

This is not to say that there aren't bargains out there. In many cases, you will stumble across incredible deals. The secret is to know what you are looking for and to have a good idea of how it should work. You can do your research by visiting with reliable used equipment dealers before you start looking.

When talking with a private party, ask them how long they have owned the equipment, why they are selling it and if they have kept any repair bills that you can see. Trust your intuition in this kind of situation; if the person seems truly interested in providing you with as much information as possible, chances are the equipment is everything they say it is or isn't. If they tell you it needs a new part, find out what the replacement part costs and ask if they would deduct it from the selling price.

When you go to see the equipment, make sure it runs. Test it out if possible, measure it to make sure it will fit into the space you have available, and decide whether you can move it yourself or will have to arrange transportation. Before buying it, try to find out whether there is a servicing outlet nearby or if you must send away for parts, which can be a time-consuming and costly project, especially on older models.

Occasionally you will run across an individual who is making payments on a piece of equipment still under warranty. This can be a great deal for you since they will probably accept a small amount of cash and let you take over the payments. Be sure to transfer ownership in writing to prevent complications if you need service under the warranty.

Going Once . . .

Auctions are an excellent way to get good bargains. Watch the business and classified sections of the newspaper for ads about upcoming auctions. The ad will include dates, the reason for the auction (liquidation or bankruptcy), location, time and a partial list of items. In most cases, there will be a preview, enabling potential buyers to view the merchandise before the bidding begins.

By all means, take advantage of the preview to inspect and select equipment you want to bid on. A fee will be required for a bidder registration number, which is held up when you make a bid so the auctioneer's spotters know who has purchased a particular item.

The two rules to remember at auctions are:

1. Cash or a personal check for the full purchase amount must be paid on the day of the auction, and
2. Don't move your hands or make significant gestures during bidding or you might find that you have purchased something you didn't want.

Leasing Equipment

Leasing is defined as a long-term agreement between two parties for the use of a specific item. The person who leases is known as the lessee, while the owner of the item is referred to as the lessor. Despite the fact that you do not own the equipment when you lease, and so can not take advantage of depreciation on it for tax purposes, there are still many benefits for the beginning business owners.

Leasing lets you try out a piece of equipment for a given period of time to determine if it is the best product for your needs. Although you are locked in, according to the terms of the lease, most lessors are flexible and will try to accommodate your requests.

Know What You Need

Of course, the way to prevent this in the first place is to be absolutely clear about what you expect the equipment to do for you. The service representative from the leasing company is well-versed in tailoring equipment to customer, so do not hesitate to ask questions about capabilities.

Most lessors offer good maintenance contracts as they want to protect their equipment. Check to see what parts and/ or labor are covered before signing the lease. The lessor should also be willing to provide technical advice at no charge, may be willing to offer installation and set-up of the equipment, and provide training, if required.

Payments can be arranged to fit your budgetary needs on a monthly, semi-annual, or annual basis. This gives you the freedom to schedule payments for peak cash-flow periods. You can also negotiate the rates and length of time of the lease to keep monthly operating expenses at a minimum.

Conditional Sales Agreement

Under the provisions of a conditional sales agreement, you become the owner of the leased goods from the agreement date. At the end of the lease period, you are required to purchase the item for a pre-established price. This is often referred to as a balloon payment and should be agreed upon by you and the lessor prior to your signing the lease.

The conditional sales agreement, unlike most other leasing contracts, gives you the tax advantage of claiming depreciation on equipment. Depreciation refers to the decrease in the value of an asset because of wear and tear over a period of time.

You are entitled to deduct depreciation, based on value when new, the estimated life of the item and the value at the end of that estimated life, from your income tax. It is best to work with your accountant on determining depreciation of fixed assets.

There is seldom a down payment, other than the first month's lease amount, required on a leased item, since leasing is generally one hundred percent financed for the term of the agreement. This frees your start-up or working capital for other uses.

True Lease Agreements

You can write off lease payments on your income tax, but only if you have a true lease contract. Under a true lease, the lessor owns the equipment at all times during the contract period. If you decided, at the end of the lease, that you wanted to buy the equipment, you would have to pay whatever purchase price was decided by the lessor.

Financial Lease

The financial lease covers a period that does not extend beyond the estimated life of the equipment. Payments must be made as stipulated on the date due and through to the end of the lease. It usually puts the responsibility and cost of maintenance on the lessee.

Operating Lease

The operating lease generally requires the lessor to handle maintenance of the equipment. It offers the option of cancelling the lease, but only if a cancellation clause has been included at the negotiating stage.

The most important aspect of leasing is not the legal name of the agreement, but the terms which are outlined in the formal lease. Have the lessor draw up a proposal for you, based on everything you have discussed in an inital meeting. If you have any trouble understanding the terms of the proposal, have your attorney review it with you. In fact, it is a definite advantage to have the final lease agreement checked by your attorney or accountant before you sign it.

The lease agreement should cover the following aspects:

- The length of the contract in months or years.
- The rate you are to be charged, which is usually a percentage of the total purchase price computed on a monthly rate.
- Your payment schedule.
- Purchase option, if applicable, at the end of the lease.
- Renewal option, if applicable, which allows you to carry the lease over for an additional period of time.
- Cancellation agreement in the event you want or need to cancel the lease.
- Maintenance stipulations (who pays for parts and labor).
- Substitution options if updated equipment is introduced and you want to take advantage of improvements.
- Any provisions particular to the lease, including tax allowances for depreciation, insurance liability in case of loss or damage, and your responsibilities in reporting a move or other major change.

Whether you decide to borrow, buy new equipment, find good used equipment, or lease, be sure to get exactly what you need to keep costs at a minimum. This is especially important during the early stages of your business when cash is bound to be tight. You can always upgrade or add to your equipment inventory as profits increase. ■

9

Selecting Professionals

From the start-up stage and as your business continues to grow and prosper, you will need the assistance of several professionals, including a lawyer, an accountant, and an insurance agent.

The best way to find a professional, according to the majority of business owners, is through personal recommendations from other entrepreneurs, especially those in businesses similar to yours, and from friends or relatives. The most important factor is that the person doing the recommending understand exactly what you will need from the professional you will be hiring.

For example, your cousin's divorce lawyer is probably not as well suited to helping you draw up a partnership agreement as the attorney who helped your friends incorporate their business.

Before making a decision, talk to several recommended professionals until you find someone who can best satisfy your needs for the business (as outlined below), and who has a fee structure you can afford. Equally important is that it be someone with whom you feel comfortable, especially during those times when you are forced to call five times a week to resolve a problem or complete a specific task. In many cases, because attorneys and accountants often work on a particular business matter in conjunction with one another, the attorney you select may be able to suggest an accountant who can properly serve your business, or vice-versa.

If you are planning to hire an attorney or an accountant, you should start "interviewing" likely candidates eight to nine months prior to the date you plan to start the business. This will give you time to find a suitable match and give them time to take care of all start-up functions, such as establishing your business form and helping you with your business plan.

What to Expect from Professional Services

Legal

You will need an attorney with broad-based expertise in business can help you with such matters as raising capital; the legal and tax ramifications and benefits of various business forms including sole proprietorship, partnership, or corporation; name clearance to ensure that you are not using a name already designated by another company; legal tips on operating in your desired location; and filing all necessary legal papers and documents needed for financing, establishing your business form and so on.

He or she will review contracts and lease agreements, and can provide support with collection problems. The lawyer you select should also be willing and able to represent you in the event that any claims are brought against you, or that you initiate any lawsuits.

Fees

Depending on your lawyer's expertise, reputation and location (metropolitan area versus small town, for example), fees will differ dramatically. In a smaller community, lawyers often charge a set rate for the job being done while "city" lawyers typically charge by the hour with fees ranging anywhere from $65 to $250 per hour.

This does not include the extraneous expenses involved, such as the $300 to $1,000 cost of incorporating (depending on the state you operate in). Additional fees also include costs such as travel and telephone incurred by the attorney in the handling of your case.

A good way to get an idea of fees in your area is to check with your local Chamber of Commerce or the state Bar Association, generally located in the capital city. The Bar Association may also be able to provide you with information about a particular attorney's reputation and expertise.

When talking with your potential attorney—and when you have found one who is compatible to your needs—always be sure to ask for an outline of expenses and find out if they are willing to notify you when the estimated fees for a particular job will be exceeded.

Accounting

The accountant you select should, early on, be able to work with you on putting together your business plan, including your projected profit and loss statements, for financing.

Down the line as your business is being established, the accountant will help you set up your books and, once in operation, should handle your tax returns, prepare financial statements, offer advice regarding tax matters, cash flow, investments to maximize the use of profits, and the tax regulations regarding employees when you are ready to hire.

Fees

As with attorneys, there is a professional association in your state capital which certifies and maintains records on the reputation and fee structures of accountants. The basis for fee structuring does vary slightly, however, with accountants. Some charge by the hour, others by the day and still others

work on a set monthly retainer, based on the estimated amount
of time they will be required to spend on your work. Fees
average between $25 and $100 hourly depending on expertise
and location.

Insurance

Before setting out on your search for an insurance agent, it is
advisable to establish your business form, learn exactly what
insurance the law in your area requires you to carry (fire,
liability, etc.), and, if hiring employees, what kind of program
you want to offer your employees. Also consider your own
needs for medical and life insurance.

There are several types of insurance you should carry for
your newsletter publishing company. General business coverage will protect against fire and theft, general liability covers
accidents or injury to anyone while they are on your work
premises, and product liability covers anyone getting hurt with
one of your products. If working out of your home, it may be
possible to add these additional types of coverage to your
existing homeowners policy at a low annual cost.

You will also need to carry workman's compensation
when you start hiring full or part-time employees, unless they
agree to work as independent contractors and take care of their
own insurance and taxes.

The insurance agent you choose should be familiar with
the needs of businesses and business owners, not just the
standard life and disability policies. Your insurance needs will
change as your business grows and expands (i.e., employee
health, workman's compensation, etc.). At that point, you may
want to consider key-person coverage to make sure your company can survive if a major partner or employee dies.

There are also a number of pension programs and stock-
option programs available in the event you want to offer

employees the incentive to increase their participation in the company in exchange for partial 'ownership' down the line.

Fees

The fees for your agent's expertise are paid from your premiums, and there should definitely not be any extra charge to you for advice or administration of your insurance policies and programs. ■

10

Taxes, Licenses, and Permits

As a business owner, you are responsible for timely report filing and payment of federal, state and local taxes. Whether you have an accountant prepare your returns, or do it yourself, the task will be made much easier if you establish a systematic record keeping system as reviewed in Chapter 14, and keep your records accurate and up-to-date.

This includes maintaining all written documents pertaining to the financial aspect of your business; invoices, bank statements, receipts of any and all business expenses, and deposit slips.

One of the easiest ways to keep control of the "paper dragon" is to set up a 9 x 12-inch manila envelope or a file folder for each of the following categories: *Paid Bills*—both personal and business; *Sales Receipts* of every product you've sold or service job performed; *Inventory* records based on ongoing inventory control and quarterly audits; *Copies of Invoices* or billing statements that are paid, with a separate file for those still due you; *Receipts* for miscellaneous cash purchases; and *Auto* and *Entertainment* receipts from travel and promotional activities.

All of these documents must be kept for at least five years to substantiate deductions claimed on your income tax returns in the event of an I.R.S. audit. Make up new file folders or envelopes at the beginning of each year and store the old ones in a safe place.

Preparing income tax returns, especially for the federal government, is not only a time-consuming task that can take you away from the important job of running your business, it has become almost an art form. Tax law is a constantly changing, complicated fact of life. It is strongly recommended that you have an accountant lined up to prepare your taxes and keep you informed of any pertinent changes during the year.

Business Deductions

The deductions that you will most likely qualify for as a business owner include operating expenses such as telephone, postage, advertising, bank service charges, travel and expense of conventions, interest, dues to professional organizations, and subscriptions to magazines pertaining to your business, among others.

If you have established your business at home, you will be able to deduct that portion of the house used exclusively for business, as well as a percentage of your costs for telephone service and utilities.

Again, because of the complexity and obscurity of many of the deductions, it is best to have a professional do your taxes to ensure you get the full benefits to which you are entitled.

The list on the next page provides an overview of the tax returns which may be applicable to your business situation. It is meant only to inform you. Filing requirements will be determined by the type of business, the legal structure (sole proprietorship, partnership or corporation), income from the business, your location, state and local laws and whether or not you have employees.

For example, as the sole proprietor of your business, you would probably only be required to file personal federal and state returns based on profit or loss, with the appropriate schedules for business expenses; pay sales, self-employment and estimated taxes, and local business license fees and sales tax.

State Income Tax

Each state has corresponding filing requirements. However, form and schedule numbers vary. Contact your State Franchise Tax Board or your accountant for details.

Federal Tax Returns

Form 1040: Income tax for Sole Proprietors, Partners or S Corporation shareholders.

Schedule C: Profit (or Loss) from Business or Profession.

Form 1065: Partnership income tax return.

Schedule K-1: Partner's share of Income, Credits, Deductions, etc.

Form 1120: Corporation tax return with applicable support schedules.

Form 2553: S Corporation Filing.

Form 1120-S: S Corporation Tax Return.

Form 1040ES: Quarterly Estimated Tax for Sole Owner or Partner.

Form 1120W: Quarterly Estimated Tax for Corporation.

Form 940: Federal Unemployment (Social Security) Tax for Sole Owner, Partner, Corporations.

Schedule SE: Annual return of self-employment tax for Sole Proprietor or Partner.

Local Taxes

Taxes will vary from city to city and county to county. However, you *may* be required to pay city income tax and local sales tax as well as real or personal property taxes. Check with your local government offices for specifics.

Licenses and Permits

To operate your business, you will need permits and licenses based on the requirements in your area and the type of business you are running. You will probably be required to obtain the following documents no matter where you live.

Local Business License. Basically this is simply a fee paid to the city or county in which you are located which allows you to operate your business in that area. Some cities will also require you to pay a percentage of your gross sales every year.

Fictitious Name Statement. This is a registration for protection of your business name. Filing the Fictitious Name Statement will also involve a city- or county-wide search to make sure you are not duplicating an existing name. See details in Naming Your Business in the next chapter.

Seller's Permit or Resale Certificate. This is required if you are going to be charging sales tax. Services are often exempt.

Health Permit. This is required only if you are preparing or distributing food in any manner. Involves an initial inspection and periodic follow-up inspections by Health Department officials.

Taxpayer Identification Number, available from the I.R.S. by filing Form SS-4, in the case of partnerships, S Corporations or Corporations. Sole Proprietors are required to have a Taxpayer Identification Number if they pay wages to one or more employees or file pension or excise tax forms.

Your local governmental offices or your attorney will be able to give you specific licenses and permits needed to conduct business in your area.

Legal Structure

As a self-employed business owner, you are required to decide on a legal form of business for tax reporting purposes. There are four basic classifications, as outlined below. If, after reviewing them, you are still unsure of which way to go, it would be advisable to talk with a lawyer about the advantages and disadvantages of each structure for your particular business.

A *Sole Proprietorship* is the easiest to establish and is the structure many small business owners choose. A proprietorship is relatively free from government regulation, as the business has no existence apart from the owner. Profits from the operation of business are treated as personal income for purposes of taxation and your proprietary interest ends when you die or dissolve the business.

The major drawback of a proprietorship is that you are personally liable for any and all claims against the business and undertake the risks of the business to the extent of all assets, whether they are used in the business or personally owned. As a sole proprietor, you will be required to file self-employment tax returns and ordinarily would have to make estimated tax payments on a quarterly basis.

A *General Partnership* is also easy to set up and administer. Since responsibilities and capitalization are usually shared by two or more partners, taxation is based on each partner's share of business income and determined by their individual tax rates. Again, claims against the business can be filed against personal assets and financial liability is shared equally by all partners.

A *Limited Partnership* can be established when one or more people are willing to invest cash or tangible property in the business with active participation in the daily operations.

However, there must be at least one general partner who carries unlimited financial liability and usually maintains a full-time managerial position within the company.

The limited partner(s) are only liable for business debts up to the amount of their investment. Although a partnership is not a taxable entity, it must figure its profit or loss and file an annual tax return, which also becomes part of the partners' personal returns.

In a *Corporation,* stock or shares in the business are sold to investors or stockholders, who then control the company. The advantage is that corporate stockholders are removed from any liability against personal assets. The most anyone can lose in the event of bankruptcy or a liability claim is their stock.

The privilege of reduced liability, however, creates paperwork (articles of incorporation and annual reports for the State Tax Commission and federal regulators), expenses (filing and licensing fees) and double taxation (the corporation is taxed on profits, while stockholders and elected officers are taxed individually on wages and/or dividend income).

Subchapter S Corporations have proven to be a real boon for small business owners who want the benefit of corporate protection from personal liability without double taxation. In a Subchapter S Corporation, a maximum of 35 stockholders (who can be family members) report their share of corporate income on individual tax returns.

The corporation itself is generally exempt from federal income tax. However, it may be required to pay a tax on excess net passive investment income, capital gains, or built-in gains. To structure your company as a Subchapter S Corporation, all of the shareholders must consent to the choice.

All businesses, regardless of size, are required to maintain detailed records and file the necessary tax returns. In a corporation, regular meetings must be held. The stockholders elect a board of directors, who establish and monitor general corporate policy. The board selects corporate officers to conduct the day-to-day operations of the business.

Sole Proprietorships are the most convenient and least complicated form of organization for new business owners, especially in the early stages. As your business grows, you will want to explore the options as a way of protecting your personal assets and increasing the potential for expansion capital. ■

11

Naming Your Business

As a pet owner, it is unlikely that you would give your German shepherd a name like "Fifi." It wouldn't suit the dog's image, nor would it be appropriate. The same principle applies to choosing a name for your business.

The name you select for your business can be a tremendous asset when it defines the kind of image you want to project. You want the name to attract and appeal to potential customers, to be easily remembered over that of the competition's, and appropriate to the type of business you are starting.

Today's consumers are constantly bombarded in advertising as they go about their daily routines with company and product names. Getting their attention, and holding it long enough for them to make an association between your business name and what you are offering, is imperative.

A memorable moniker can mean the difference between continued growth or a mediocre response from an audience victimized by information overload. (It is, of course, important to remember that ultimate success is dependent on well-designed advertising, careful planning, and quality products and/or service.)

Selecting a Name for your Newsletter

A good name should tell your readers exactly what to expect. Lively titles attract attention and are memorable. You don't want to be so lively that your name sounds "cute," but you don't want to choose a name so serviceable that it sounds flat.

The California Carvers' Guild has a newsletter called *The Log*. A financial analyst named Howard Ruff publishes a newsletter called *Ruff Times*.

The American Retail Travel Agents have a newsletter called *ARTAFacts*. If you look through directories of newsletters in your local library, you will see thousands of names and probably be able to come up with a good one of your own.

Subtitles

Good subtitles make your purposes and readership more clear. Names and subtitles should go hand in hand. You may have seen *EnergyNews* sent to you with your gas bill. It's subtitle says, "A pipeline and gas utilities bi-weekly, edited for management, users and producers, and reporting on supplies, prices, regulations and construction in the natural gas industry." Not all subtitles are this long, but this one certainly lets its readers know what it's about.

Brainstorming

Start by making a list of all the positive aspects of your business that you can think of and call on friends and relatives to provide as many as they can come up with. Write down all the possibilities, no matter how funny or unusual they seem. A handy tool for business naming is the thesaurus, which will give you a vast number of options for commonplace names. Consider everything that springs forth from your imagination.

When you have created a list of 15, 25 or more likely candidates, get together with a group of supportive friends and family members and have a brainstorming session to either pick one of the choices you have come up with or to develop something from the ideas listed. Chances are that within a few hours, you will have a name for your business.

Catchy names are fun to design. However, make sure it isn't so off-beat, cute or trendy as to risk slipping into obscurity as time passes. For instance, the astrology craze of the 1970s resulted in thousands of businesses being named after stars, birth signs or related celestial phenomena. As the trend faded, a number of business were able to change their focus *and* their name to survive. Other, however, were so closely associated by their astrological name that they were forced, unfortunately, to close.

The Fictitious Name Statement

You are required to file a fictitious name statement with the County Clerk's office where you will be basing the business. While there, you should be able to do a county-wide name check on the spot to see if there are any other businesses in the region using the name you have selected. The filing fee is $10 to $20, depending on where you live, and must be done within 30 days after you officially open your business.

It will also be necessary to publish the fictitious name in your local newspaper, which will cost between $25 and $50, depending on the circulation of the paper. The County Clerk's office will advise you about specific requirements in your area.

If you are starting a business that will be operating in a broader market, statewide or nationally, it is important to have your attorney do a name clearance investigation, which can take from three days to three weeks.

Your Visual Image

After you have selected a name that reflects your business image, the next step is translating it into a visual symbol or logo (logotype) to serve as the signature piece for your business. Often this involves creating a visual interpretation of your company name, but in other cases, a graphic symbol or trademark is designed to serve as identificationon your sign, business cards and other promotional material.

Some established corporate trademarks are so familiar that, in many cases, you can immediately identify the company even without seeing or hearing its name.

A good example of this includes the logo of the dog with his head cocked to one side. The accompanying copy reads, "His Master's Voice," and it's a good bet that you recognize this as the logo for RCA. Another effective logo is the avant garde apple that identifies Apple computer products.

If you do not have the graphic skills necessary to design a logo with impact, get in touch with your nearest art association (listed in the phone book or available through local art supply shops or galleries) or call a nearby college or university. Ask the head of the art department if your design can be given as a class assignment or whether they would recommend a student to do the job for a small fee.

It will give students practical application and the design can be used later in their portfolio. You can offer a prize or a fee for the best design and the students will undoubtedly meet the challenge with enthusiasm and give you a number of good samples and ideas from which to choose.

Selecting a Typeface

Save sample logos and advertisements that use a typeface you like. Type, created either by a professional typesetting machine or on a desktop publishing computer, is an extremely important element of logo design and can also pinpoint the precise image you hope to express. Type not only presents the basic message, it can play a powerful role in the overall appearance of your logo and can actually create atmosphere. We have provided a chart on Page 97 of some of the more popular typefaces available.

When deciding on a typeface for your logo, visit print shops or typesetting studios and look at their typeface books. They offer both the usual, functional varieties as well as a selection of unique typefaces that can really dress up your logo by portraying a specific personality such as dignified, fun, feminine, powerful, classic, ultra-modern, etc., in a subtle way.

Historically, in developing business names, simplicity has scored the highest points. The name you choose should be short, to the point, and easy for consumers to pronounce.

Have the logo and your business information (address, phone number, etc.) set in more than the one typeface so that you can see how they will look when printed. Also ask to have them set in both small (10-point to 12-point for business cards) and larger (20- to 24-point for letterhead) versions. Once typeset, you will be able to make a final decision about which typeface suits the image you want to project.

Typesetters generally have a minimum fee based on the amount of time they spend on a job and this can vary anywhere from $15 per hour in a small city to $50 per hour in a business area and as high as $100 per hour in major metropolitan areas, so be sure to shop around.

Word processors or independent desktop publishers can also provide a variety of typefaces and formats at less expense. Since you will only be having a few words typeset, the time and cost required to set them in several different styles should certainly be affordable.

Business Cards and Stationery

The typeface and logo you eventually choose will be used on your letterhead, in your display and telephone advertising, on all promotional materials, including flyers, brochures, and announcements, on your sign and on statements and invoices.

It will also be used on your business cards, one of the most inexpensive and convenient ways to inform people about your service or product. Once you have had them printed, be generous. Give them to everyone you meet and always be sure to carry a supply wherever you go.

Most fast-print copy centers are prepared to help you if you decide not to design your own business cards and stationery. They have samples of business forms, letterhead and cards with various styles to choose from. Make sure that your company name, logo, address, and phone number are included where necessary. When someone looks at your card or letterhead, it must tell them instantly who you are, what your business is and where they can find you. ■

Sample Typefaces

Helvetica Medium Conden
ABCDEFGHIJKLMNOPQR
abcdefghijklmnopqrstuvwx

Helvetica Black Italic
ABCDEFGHIJKLMNO
abcdefghijklmnopqr

ITC Korinna Medium
ABCDEFGHIJKLM
abcdefghijklmnop

ITC Korinna Bold
ABCDEFGHIJKLM
abcdefghijklmnopq

ITC Korinna Extra Bold
ABCDEFGHIJKL
abcdefghijklmnop

ITC Korinna Heavy
ABCDEFGHIJK
abcdefghijklmn

Melior Roman
ABCDEFGHIJKL
abcdefghijklmno

Melior Italic
ABCDEFGHIJKL
abcdefghijklmno

Melior Bold
ABCDEFGHIJKL
abcdefghijklmno

Linotext Roman
ABCDEFGHIJK
abcdefghijklmnopqrst

ITC Serif Gothic Light
ABCDEFGHIJKLMN
abcdefghijklmnop

ITC Bauhaus Medium
ABCDEFGHIJKLMN
abcdefghijklmnop

ITC Bauhaus Bold
ABCDEFGHIJKLM
abcdefghijklmno

Eurostile Roman
ABCDEFGHIJKL
abcdefghijklmnop

Eurostile Bold
ABCDEFGHIJKL
abcdefghijklmnop

Eurostile Extended
ABCDEFGHIJKL
abcdefghijklmno

Eurostile Extended Bold
ABCDEFGHIJKLM
abcdefghijklmnopq

Helvetica Bold Outline
ABCDEFGHIJKLMNOP
abcdefghijklmnopqrstu

Helvetica Medium Roman
ABCDEFGHIJKLMNOPQ
abcdefghijklmnopqrstuv

Helvetica Bold Italic
ABCDEFGHIJKLMNOP
abcdefghijklmnopqrst

Times Roman
ABCDEFGHIJKL
abcdefghijklmnop

Times Italic
ABCDEFGHIJKLM
abcdefghijklmnopqr

Optima Roman
ABCDEFGHIJKLM
abcdefghijklmnop

Optima Italic
ABCDEFGHIJKLM
abcdefghijklmnop

Optima Bold
ABCDEFGHIJKLM
abcdefghijklmnop

Pabst Extra Bold
ABCDEFGHIJ
abcdefghijklm

Pabst Extra Bold It
ABCDEFGHIJK
abcdefghijklm

Palatino Roman
ABCDEFGHIJKL
abcdefghijklmno

Palatino Italic
ABCDEFGHIJKL
abcdefghijklmnopq

Palatino Bold
ABCDEFGHIJK
abcdefghijklmn

Yupital Script
ABCDE FGHIJKL
abcdefghijklmnopqrstuv

ITC Tiffany Roman
ABCDEFGHIJK
abcdefghijklmno

ITC Tiffany Heavy
ABCDEFGHIJ
abcdefghijklm

12

Developing a Business Plan

Developing your business plan is the most important process you will undertake in your career as an entrepreneur, regardless of the size or type of business you have decided to start.

A well-thought-out business plan will serve as a blueprint while your idea turns into a recognizable entity and as it grows into a stable and profitable venture. Too often we hear former small business owners say they probably could have made a success of their business if they had only known what to expect from the beginning . . . and that is where the business plan comes in.

Unfortunately, too many new entrepreneurs are unfamiliar with the importance of planning or they consider themselves an exception and feel they can succeed by winging it or dealing with problems as they arise. Not so!

Every business, whether a large commercial or a small home-based venture, needs to analyze its potential, examine strengths and weaknesses, and determine the future of the company. It works for the major corporations and it will work for you, especially once you become involved in the day-to-day operations of the business! Having a business plan will give you the freedom to follow the steps you have carefully laid out with regard to budgeting, the success ratio of a product or service, the hiring of employees and other growth decisions.

The Advantages of Planning

Once you have made the decision to become a business owner, you must devise a specific statement that clearly outlines *what* you plan to do, *when* you plan to do it and *how* you will accomplish the short and long-term goals.

Not only will this keep you on track, it will serve as an indicator to others of your sincerity and knowledge when you go out to find start-up or expansion capital, and will serve as the foundation of your financing proposal.

The other advantage is that the actual task of putting your business plan together will help you define and clarify every step of your concept and, if done in a conscientious and objective manner, will point out potential trouble spots that can be addressed before they become major problems.

If all the necessary components are covered, it will put your business on the road to profit. It is a sure bet that, down the road, if you find your business is not generating the income you had originally projected, this is because you didn't include one or more of the basic business plan requirements.

Not a Guessing Game

Like any other major project, preparing a business plan involves time and research. It shouldn't be a guessing game. It will be necessary to ask yourself some very specific questions and to answer them thoughtfully and honestly. The business plan is your foundation, so build it carefully to ensure that it works at optimum efficiency for your needs. And make sure it is typed, orderly, and good looking so you, and others, recognize its importance in your professional scheme of things.

An important aspect to remember is that your business plan is not cast in stone. In fact, one of the wonderful things about a business plan is that it invites change and revisions as your business changes. This makes it a companion in your success and, by reviewing it regularly, a partner in your progress.

Case History

A.J. Mann started her newsletter *Doll House* on a bet. A friend dared her to start a business for $25, which he offered to invest in the venture.

"After thinking about it for a few days, I realized the best option was to capitalize on my doll collection and take out a classified ad in an antique tabloid that reaches 250,000 on the West Coast. The ad cost me $21.50 for three lines stating:

Doll House, the newsletter for serious doll collectors.
Interviews, articles, facts and fiction.
$15 yr/10 issues. P.O. Box 3845, S.B., 93130.

Within two weeks, A.J. had 60 subscribers and found herself in a position of having to create the first issue!

The best way to approach your business plan is to take paper and pen and devote a few hours to coming up with some hard answers. Of course, you will want to condense your answers to fit into specific segments within the plan, including (in order of appearance) Concept and Feasibility, Legal Structure, Product or Service, Customer Base, Marketing and Production Goals, Personnel (your resumé and Entrepreneurial Profile and those of any other key personnel), and Financial Statements.

It is advisable to start each segment on a separate page and to create a Table of Contents to place in the front. Be sure it is neatly typed, well written and organized, and bound in a report folder to preserve it and give it a professional quality, especially when using it as a "sales" tool to convince lenders.

Starting to Build Your Business Plan

The first question you must ask yourself is, "Why am I interested in this particular business?" Probably your answer will be something to the effect of wanting to be your own boss and making money . . . Independence and Income.

This answer is fine as a personal goal, but it isn't going to be good enough if you are planning to approach potential lenders for funding. They will want to see an overview of your business concept, why you are convinced it will be successful, and where it fits in the scheme of similar businesses in your town or city.

The next question you must address is, "What is my product or service?" This may seem like a ridiculous question since you know your product is gift baskets or your service is catering, local sightseeing tours or whatever, but it goes deeper. Your written response will include details about the service or a description of your product (preferably positive), and focusing on why customers will be inclined to purchase from you.

Additional questions to analyze should include:

- Why do I believe there is a need for my product or service?
- How do I plan to develop my business over the next five years?
- How much will I charge to ensure value to the customer and profit for myself?
- Who are my suppliers?
- Who are my customers?
- What equipment do I need to start the business?
- How much inventory and supplies do I need for start-up?
- What will it cost?
- Who is my competition and where are they located?
- What are they offering and how can I improve my offer to attract customers?

- What changes are occurring in my marketing area which will affect my business in the future?
- What are my estimated sales figures for each of the next five years (a "guesstimate" based on researching similar businesses in the area)?
- How will I advertise and promote my business (including estimated costs of doing so)?
- How and where is my product going to be manufactured?
- What is involved in the production—materials, labor, costs?
- Where will my service be performed?
- What equipment is required for my service (costs for leasing versus purchasing)?
- What are other overhead expenses (rent, employees, etc.)?
- How many people will be involved in the business and what are their qualifications?
- If I don't have employees, am I qualified to run the business myself? Will I need outside assistance?

By talking with people in similar businesses, suppliers and direct competitors, as well as your local Chamber of Commerce, you will gather a great deal of information, both positive and negative, about your potential business. People love to talk about their success and, if you ask in the right way, their failures.

Become an investigative reporter for a few days while preparing to write your business plan and it's guaranteed that you will obtain plenty of good, solid information. A SCORE representative through the Small Business Information Bureau can also offer assistance, or give you resources that will help you develop a realistic business plan.

Trade associations, listed in reference books available at your local library, can provide you with invaluable details on industry facts and figures, such as the percentage of gross sales that should be spent on advertising, the percentage that is typically paid for rent in your particular business, and how to price your product or service, for example.

The final item to include in this section of your business plan, when and if presenting it for financing, is a personal resumé, designed to emphasize your general business management experience and your expertise within your specific area.

Describe the job duties for every job you have held, including any special aspects that pertain directly to your business. If you can not prepare the resumé, it is worth the $25 to $40 to have it done professionally.

Show me a person with an obsession about succeeding and a solid business plan and I'll show you a good risk.

Anonymous Loan Officer

The Financial Pages

Once you have written your overview and description sheets, it is time to get down to numbers. This is the key to your business plan and, unfortunately, the area where many entrepreneurs get bogged down. But without an understanding about the numbers involved, you can never expect to be a good manager and really shouldn't be surprised if you run into money problems within the first year.

Again, utilizing the resources indicated above—Chamber of Commerce, trade associations, etc.—you will need to work up your financial pages to include the following components, which most lenders will want to see projected from one and five years.

- *Projected operating expenses.* Includes materials, advertising, salaries for employees or outside labor, and other expenses directly related to the cost of doing business.
- *Estimate of gross (before tax) sales revenue.* Based on research figures from trade associations and what the local market dictates, if the business is not yet operating or, if open, how many items or hours of service you plan to sell, and the average price.
- *How you arrived at the figures for these statements.* Generally you would base your figures on assumptions made about the number of months of operation, estimated number of sales, and the average amount versus the cost of each sale.
- *Cost of equipment and furnishings.* Get estimated quotes, whether planning to purchase or lease these items.
- *Cost of materials.* For production, if applicable, or maintenance of equipment needed to run the business.
- *Additional operating expenses.* Rent, telephone and other utilities, business taxes and license fees, office supplies, even decorating costs and a category called "other" to provide a cushion for unexpected expenses.
- *Balance sheet.* Shows assets, such as equipment and operating capital you already have, and liabilities or debts and expenses (if the business has not yet started, this would be a personal balance sheet indicating your net worth, listing all possessions of any value, plus cash, stock and other holdings minus all financial responsibilities).
- *Leasehold improvements.* If you are planning to rent a commercial location or redesign a room within your home strictly for business, estimate cleaning and restoration costs in this statement.

By investing the time and energy into this portion of the business plan, you will absorb the numbers into your consciousness and be able to recognize, at a glance, when your costs exceed your profit margin or when you are in a position to start expanding.

If money matters are absolutely beyond your comprehension at this point, it would pay to hire someone to work along with you in developing the financial pages of the plan. There are business consultants and accountants who will probably charge you a substantial amount, or you can approach the accounting or business department of the nearest college and see if there is a qualified student available to help you.

No matter whom you find to assist you, however, be sure that you stay involved in the process ... the discipline and hard work will guarantee success. ■

13

Financing Your Business

Starting your business without having sufficient capital is setting yourself up for problems from the beginning. Undercapitalization is cited as one of the major reasons why businesses do not succeed; however, this simply boils down to bad planning.

If you research and record all the goals, marketing data, equipment and supply requirements, and financial needs of your venture before actually opening the doors, you will be able to see at a glance how much you need to get going, and *why you need it*. That way, there will be no surprises and no reason that your business should suffer from lack of capitalization.

It is important to have the financial resources to cover all your preliminary planning and start-up costs, including expenses incurred to research the feasibility of your business and expenses required to set up shop, from equipment and supplies to advertising and utility set-up charges, in addition to a surplus to carry you over personally until the business becomes productive. The Cash Flow Statement and Projected Expense Charts provided in Chapter 7 will help you determine these expenses.

If, after drawing up your business plan (Chapter 12), you find that your personal resources are not enough to open the business, there are other options available.

The four most common methods include starting the business on a part-time basis while holding a full-time job to cover expenses, taking on a limited partner, going to friends or family members for the money you need, or applying for a loan through a commercial lender or the Small Business Administration (SBA). There are, of course, pros and cons to each of these options.

Moonlighting

Starting your business on a part-time or "moonlighting" basis is a decision that must be made based on the nature of the business. If you are planning to capitalize on your skills in upholstering, for example, you should have no trouble building up the business at night and on weekends.

It is perfectly feasible to start small, using your garage or a spare room as your production facility and purchasing an answering machine for potential customers to leave a message while you are at your regular job. When you get home, you simply call them back to discuss prices and arrange a time when it is convenient to pick up the piece of furniture to be upholstered.

On the other hand, if you are planning to start a temporary help agency, for example, it would be in your best interest to go into it on a full-time, dedicated basis, as your potential customers are going to want fast results and will call someone else if they are even slightly discouraged, such as getting a recorded message when they call.

Moonlighting will work with some businesses, but before exploring it as an option you must figure out if your limited availability will affect your credibility, if you really have the time and energy to work at a regular job and try to build a business (not to mention family responsibilities) and whether your ultimate goal is to be self-employed or just to earn a few extra dollars to supplement your base income.

Taking on a Partner

A limited partner is one who will put up the money you need and step into the background to let you run the business the way you see fit. You must be sure, however, to have your lawyer draw up a precise partnership agreement that covers every eventuality. Partnerships are typically entered into with the best intentions and the unwavering belief that the business will be successful.

Since this is not always the case—and even if it were—it is a businesslike move to ensure that such aspects as decision making, distribution of profits and losses, contributions of partners, and handling disputes and changes are outlined and approved by all the partners.

> *Money brings some happiness.*
> *But, after a certain point,*
> *it just brings more money.*
>
> **Neil Simon**

"Friendly" Financing

The third option, raising capital through friends or family members, is probably one of the most often exercised methods. The advantage of getting a loan from a personal contact is that they know you, undoubtedly trust your ability to make the business go and won't require much in the way of substantiating paperwork, such as complex loan applications, financial statements, etc. In addition, you will most likely be able to negotiate a low interest rate on the loan.

The major disadvantage, according to entrepreneurs who have taken this route, is if the friendly lender decides they want to provide input on the care and maintenance of your business. This problem, however, can be eliminated by a "cards-on-the-table" discussion prior to accepting the loan. In other words, choose your investor carefully!

The second problem has to do with repayment of the loan. Even though you have a loose agreement in writing with your lender, because of friendship or family ties there may come a point when Uncle Bill needs that $10,000 *tomorrow* to take care of a personal obligation. You can't possibly come up with the money overnight, Uncle Bill gets angry and that whole side of the family turns against you.

The flip side of the coin is if the business fails and you are unable to pay Uncle Bill or your old college pal the $5,000 she put up. These are unpleasant situations, so you must be sure in the beginning to think about the importance of the relationship you have with the potential lender, how the best and the worst of situations would affect the situation, and whether you then could justify asking for money.

Commercial Lenders

If you are not able to, or decide against approaching friends or relatives for financial assistance, the next step is a bank, a savings and loan or a credit union. Before approaching any of these commercial lenders you must have carefully developed your business plan, which will include the following documents:

1. A resumé or statement outlining your background and capability to operate the business, plus a similar statement about any key employees or partners in the business.
2. A statement of business and personal goals.
3. A description of the business, including research of the market for your product or service.
4. Details on how the business is going to be structured (sole proprietorship, partnership, corporation, non-profit status).

5. A projection of profit and loss for a minimum of one year, which forces you to do your homework and investigate how similar businesses in similar locations are doing.
6. An outline of how much money you need—and why—to keep the business solvent and to support yourself and your family for at least a year.

In addition, you will be required to provide a personal balance sheet which lists your assets, such as property, a car, etc., and liabilities like your mortgage payments, credit card debts, etc., and a credit application which outlines your personal financial history (so they can make a determination on your ability to pay back the loan). The lender will follow through by requesting a credit report from an independent agency, such as TRW, to help them make their decision.

The main thing to remember when applying for a loan with a commerical institution is that lenders aren't as concerned about how much money they loan as they are about how and when they are going to get the money back!

Presenting Your Case

Once you have your business plan and other paperwork prepared, decide which lending association you want to approach. Certainly, if you have a stable record with a checking or savings account at your regular bank or S&L, that is the place to try first. Set up an appointment with the bank manager or loan officer to make your request and explain why you feel your business venture is worth their investment.

Be aware, however, that banks are more likely to provide you with a loan payable within five or ten years, as opposed to savings & loans, which are more interested in long-term loans, such as for mortgages. Credit unions operate in a similar manner to banks, however, you generally have to be a member.

If you do belong to a credit union, it could be your best bet as they offer lower interest rates and can be more flexible in their determinations.

If, for some reason, you do not want to run a loan through your bank, consider talking with other local small business owners. Very often, they can steer you to a regional, often independently owned bank or S&L which is empathetic to and supportive of new businesses. In that case, proceed as mentioned above and arrange a meeting with the manager or loan officer.

Paying Back the Loan

When you apply for financing, whether through a friend, relatives, lending institution, a venture capitalist or under any other type of arrangement, the burden of proof as it relates to repayment rests with you.

No one would knowingly grant a loan to an individual or a business that they had doubts about. As a borrower, your responsibility is to show that you will be able to pay back the loan according to the terms agreed to by you and the lender. This can be done through a credit history that indicates you have a sense of responsibility.

Present your case in a friendly yet professional manner. Be realistic and honest about your needs. Do not underbid because of fear that you will not get a loan if you ask for too much. It is always better to start with a higher figure than you actually need so you have a strong negotiating edge.

In addition, most lenders have a pretty good idea about start-up and operating costs of new businesses and are much less likely to give you, and risk losing, a small loan for a business they know calls for more capital. They will be more willing to work with you if you are realistic and obviously knowledgeable about your needs.

If, after your first try, the answer is no, ask for reasons why you are being turned down so you can restructure your presentation. Turn opposition into a learning tool to redefine and polish your material and to develop new negotiating strategies. There are always other potential lenders you can approach, and the law of averages dictates that you will get your loan if the idea is solid and it is apparent that you have researched the feasibility of starting a business in your particular area.

The Small Business Administration

The Small Business Administration (SBA) often goes where no other lender will tread and, as such, is a lender of last resort. It is a government agency that is well known for providing financing to entrepreneurs who have been repeatedly turned down by commercial lenders, which in fact, you generally must do before the SBA will consider backing you.

After your loan request with a commercial institution has been denied, you can file an application with the nearest branch of the SBA. It is a good idea to make an appointment with a Service Corps of Retired Executives (SCORE) representative, who volunteers his or her time to the SBA-SCORE program to advise new and established business owners. Your SCORE representative will be able to lead you through the complex paperwork required by the SBA before they make a decision.

In addition, the SCORE volunteers are usually straightforward, knowledgeable men and women who will walk through your business plans with you and offer constructive suggestions. Once the paperwork is completed, a commercial lender will make the loan under the SBA Lender Certification Program, knowing that the government is willing to insure it.

We recommend this option only after you have been turned down by three or more banks, because of the time factor involved in gaining approval and also because of the extensive follow-up reports required of SBA. It is, however, a viable option and one that has helped thousands of dedicated entrepreneurs realize their goals.

Venture Capitalists

Money is available to businesses that are already established and seeking working or expansion capital from groups of investors known as *venture capitalists*. These groups can vary from a few local businessmen with money to invest to major investment companies connected with large corporations or financial organizations.

Venture capital is not like a straightforward business loan. It is usually dependent on a minimum $100,000 investment and, therefore, is not suited to every business situation. Typically, venture capitalists are interested in companies that have a track record, a proven position in the market and a solid growth projection.

But, like a bank or other lending association, venture capitalists want to see a written business plan and a prospectus of future projections. They are looking at your background, the market, the kind of funding you want and your past financial record.

Since venture capitalists are looking to earn from ten to fifteen percent on their investment over a relatively short period, they will want to spend a great deal of time talking with you and your associates, customers and suppliers.

Before considering venture capital, we advise discussing it carefully with an attorney who can help you investigate different groups to figure out the best investment structure, and who can work with their attorney on drawing up an agreement that protects you. Many venture capitalists will want to own part of your company.

This is an option to be considered only when your company is well established and undergoing rapid growth pains and should be approached with great understanding of the situation.

Other Options for Financing

Loan companies, such as Household Finance and Beneficial Finance, are a source of funding. However, interest rates are high and they will generally want to have substantial collateral, such as the equity in your house, on record before making a loan.

Insurance companies. Your insurance carrier may be willing to make an investment in your small business, using your insurance policy as collateral. Or, you may even have enough cash value in your policy, depending on the face amount, to provide substantial start-up capital. If this is the case, you will only be required to pay quarterly or semi-annual interest payments on the cash value you have taken out.

In this instance, a factoring company 'buys' your accounts receivable and advances you a percentage of the full amount due. This is a viable option for well-established service companies that work on a billing basis.

Co-signer. If you have a relative or friend who is already an established business owner or, at least, a homeowner with a solid credit rating, it might be worth your while to ask if they would co-sign on a loan application with you. Although you are still responsible for repayment of the loan, the bank is assured that, in the event you default for any reason, the co-signer will guarantee the obligation. It is often difficult to find someone who will do this, but again it doesn't hurt to ask, especially if it is a last resort.

Starting Small

Even if you know your particular business is valid and that you have the ability to make it succeed, be certain that your business plan is realistic. If you have chosen to start a business on a grand scale but have minimal capital and little business experience, it may be best to begin a smaller, less elaborate operation at first.

You'll require less "seed money" and put yourself in a low-risk position while learning the ropes and seeing if you can handle all the variables of business ownership while making it grow.

Smaller businesses have proven to be a great way to learn the successful methods, as well as a vehicle for ironing out the many small details that are often overlooked until you actually start taking care of day-to-day situations. The profits you gain from a smaller venture can be used to expand or invest in bigger business ideas. And, an added bonus is that when you are ready to approach investors or lending institutions, you will be able to show them that you already have a solid track record and a working knowledge of business procedures.

---

*The journey of a thousand miles
begins with a single step.*

Chinese Proverb

What To Do When Asking for Money

Be sure to ask. This may seem like a gross statement of the obvious, but you would be amazed at the number of small business owners we talk to who never ask because they are afraid of being turned down.

Unless you are independently wealthy and pursuing your business as a humanitarian effort, it is unlikely that you are in a position to run your business and earn enough money to support you, your family and the operation—especially during the first year. Remember the old adage: It takes money to make money.

If you run a low-budget business you will probably get a low-budget response. If you are determined to make it work, be sure you have sufficient capital to make it work the right way.

Fear *is* often a factor: "I don't want to ask, in case they say no." Well, that's the worst thing that can happen. But, if you persevere and are serious about your venture, someone will inevitably say yes!

And don't overlook friends and family; they can be your most ardent cheerleaders and supporters if you have given them reason in the past to believe you are responsible and determined to succeed.

Know how much you need.   Lenders are familiar with the financial demands of business operation and will respect your request if you have obviously done your homework and can talk sensibly about your needs.

Be direct and confident.   If you believe in your business and in your ability to make it work, others will be convinced. Never apologize for mistakes you feel you have made in the past and do not present the pathetic picture of someone who could make everything work if they just had enough money.

Simply present the facts honestly, even if it includes revealing an error in judgment you have made somewhere along the line, and assure the lender that they will be making a smart decision by investing in you.

Think positively. If you need $50,000, ask for $50,000. Never underestimate the potential to provide. Even if you are approaching family members, you may be surprised to find that dear Cousin Fred has a $250,000 nest egg socked away. Anyway, it is easier to negotiate and deal with one lender for a single amount than it is to keep paperwork and relationships strong with several, all of whom have contributed to the pot.

Ask again. If they trusted you once and you have lived up to the stipulations of the contract, ask again and that goes for commercial lending institutions as well as friends and relatives. A proven record is what it's all about and if you have established yours, keep it active.

Know when to borrow. If you have worked out your business plan and know you can survive while getting the business off the ground, start exploring your financing options ahead of time. Don't wait until the fifth month rolls around when you will be forced to act frantically and accept a less-than-favorable situation. The same theory applies if your business is already established. By examining your financial position on a regular basis, you will be able to project how much you will need at a given point for expansion purposes. Be prepared.

Don't borrow if it is not necessary. Many businesses can be started for under $500. This is called "starting on a shoestring" and can be done with a variety of businesses. Services, for example, often rely strictly on the owner's knowledge and expertise and can be set up quickly and inexpensively.

If this is the case with the business you have in mind, then try to avoid borrowing capital. It can be an expensive and timely proposition. In addition, if, after a projected period of time, the business is showing the kind of profit you can work with while growing, then the smart decision is to utilize the funds and put them back into the operation.

Establishing Credit

Is it possible to get a loan even if you have never established credit? Yes, it is. Many people still prefer to pay cash, rather than incur high interest charges on loans or credit cards. They can still qualify for a loan based on personal assets or by having a friend or relative with a good credit rating who is willing to co-sign. This puts the obligation on the co-signer, so be sure the terms of the loan are clearly spelled out in a written agreement to the satisfaction of everyone involved in the transaction.

However, if your personal assets are minimal and you cannot find a co-signer, the best bet is to put off starting the business for four to six months while you establish credit. The best place to start is with a major department store such as Sears or J.C. Penney.

They issue credit cards based on a very simple examination of your income and employment history. Charge about $100 worth of merchandise when you receive the card and pay it off according to the schedule provided. Within a few months, you will have proven yourself to be credit worthy, which will greatly improve your chances of getting a loan from a lending institution.

Another way to establish credit—and credibility—is to open a checking account at the bank you have decided to approach for a loan. They generally require a minimum deposit of between $50 and $100. Make it a point to meet the branch manager and/or the loan officer and to establish an ongoing relationship with them by stopping by to say hello when you are in the bank.

Within a few months, apply for a small personal loan, working with your new acquaintance, of course. Make your payments according to the prearranged schedule. Then when you are ready to request a more substantial amount of money to cover your start-up expenses, you will be recognized as a customer with a loan history at that institution. ■

14

Record Keeping: Your Business Lifeline

The motivating factor in any business is profit, which can be explained as the money left over after all the bills, for everything from supplies to rent and salaries to taxes, are paid.

Building a profitable business is not something that can be left to chance; it must be planned and a systematic method of record keeping must be developed to help you control income and expenses.

You should expect that during the early days of your business, your profits are going to be minimal as you become established. But it is possible, with even simple record keeping procedures, to prepare yourself for lean periods and control day-to-day expenses to ensure that you are, at least, breaking even.

In addition, financial records are required for tax purposes and dealing with them systematically can eliminate an incredibly overwhelming task at tax time.

Record Keeping Can Be Simple

Some people cringe at the thought of record keeping or feel it is a waste of valuable time. Usually, these attitudes are based on a lack of knowledge and the feeling that it is an overwhelming task. There is, however, no other way to analyze your cash flow and make sure you are pricing products or services high enough to realize a profit.

In actuality, record keeping is not such a complicated process. If you have ever balanced a checkbook or planned a household budget, you were basically doing several of the same steps that are necessary for implementing a bookkeeping system for your business. And the good news is that keeping your records does not have to be either complicated or time consuming.

We know of entrepreneurs who opt for total simplicity by using the "shoebox" method—every sales record, receipt for expenses and bank statement gets tossed into a box. This system has two distinct drawbacks. One may not become apparent until tax time, when you attempt to wade through the paper to prepare your tax return. (If you hire an accountant to do your taxes, it shouldn't come as a surprise if an additional "combat fee" has been added to the bill.)

The other, more critical drawback is that it is virtually impossible to maintain an accurate picture of your financial situation when you stockpile, rather than record, business transactions. In order to understand your cash flow, it is important to be able to see what monies have come in, what you have paid out, current balances and outstanding debts.

In fact, you should be able to answer the following questions with just a quick review of your records:

- What was my income last year (or week, or month)?
- What were my expenses?
- How do income and expenses compare with last year (or week, or month)?
- What was my profit (or loss) last year (or week, or month)?
- Where can I cut back on expenses?
- Who and how much do I currently owe on outstanding debts?
- Who owes me money and how much?
- What are my assets, liabilities and net worth?

- Is my inventory in line with demand?
- How much cash do I have available? How much credit?
- Am I able to pay myself this month (week)?
- Are my figures in line with projected financial goals?

The primary documents you need, to be able to answer most of these questions, are your Cash Journal, a Balance Sheet, and a Bank Reconciliation. A simple single-entry system, as indicated on the following pages, in which to record disbursements (cash paid out) and receipts (cash taken in) forms the base of your record keeping.

If you can organize your kitchen,
you can organize your life.

Dr. Louis Parrish

The Double-Entry System

Your accountant will probably utilize a double-entry system, which involves recording each transaction twice; once as a debit (simply the left column of the ledger) and once as a credit (the right column of the ledger). For example, if you were to sell a product for $100, the transactions recorded in a double-entry system would be as follows:

The $100 would be written as a *credit* in your Sales account, since merchandise is going out of the business and $100 would be recorded as a *debit* in your Cash account since money was coming into the business (see page 123).

This is a complex and time-consuming process that is often best left to an accountant, as he or she will need the information to create a monthly Trial Balance and other financial statements, including your year-end tax reports.

Single-Entry Bookkeeping

You can, however, have your accountant's office set up a simple single-entry system for you which will tie in directly with their requirements. Or, check out the standardized bookkeeping systems, which provide all the necessary forms and documents in a bound book, stocked by stationery stores.

One of the most widely accepted, ready-made systems is the *Dome Simplified Monthly Bookkeeping Record*. It contains forms for recording monthly income and expenses, summary sheets from which you can create a Balance Sheet and listings of legal deductions for income tax reporting. Instructions are included.

In addition, the trade association for your field should be able to provide you with systems developed exclusively for use in the industry, which you can use 'as-is' or adapt according to specific circumstances within your business.

The final method is to purchase a Cash Journal book and set up your own monthly system, as outlined later in this chapter, for *Office Assistance*, a small typing service, which has been operating for one month. Any of the above-mentioned methods are acceptable, as long as you understand the entry process and can "read" the results.

Make Record Keeping a Daily Task

The easiest way (short of paying someone else) to be sure your records are kept up-to-date is to incorporate the task into your daily or weekly routine. Many small business owners make it a habit to enter their sales, expenses and other financial information at the end of each working day. It keeps them continually aware of their financial situation and ensures that there will never be any cash-flow surprises.

The process probably takes no more than fifteen minutes for normal transactions, but will save hours of pencil-pushing and frustration down the line. And, more important, you'll know where you stand financially.

Debit & Credit in Bookkeeping

Debits include:	*Credits include:*
• Cash receipts	• Cash payments
• Purchases	• Sales of services or merchandise
• Expenses, such as rent and wages	• Earnings, including interest earned

---

Setting Up the Books

Using Office Assistance, a secretarial service, as an example, we can examine the various elements required for basic record-keeping duties.

Bill Miller, president of Office Assistance, has been in business for one month. Two months ago, he opened a new business bank account with $10,000, his start-up capital from a personal savings account.

At the same time, he rented a small office in a downtown building for $350 a month, but had to pay the first month's rent and a deposit of the last month's rent, for a total outlay of $700.

His fictitious name statement, which he got approved through the local County Clerk's office, ran $10, and publishing it in a regional newspaper was $45.

The initial month's lease and a deposit on a state-of-the-art typewriter cost him $275, plus $50 for a maintenance agreement. However, he will own the $2,000 typewriter when his payment schedule is completed.

He found a brand new calculator at a garage sale for $25 and is going to use a desk, table, lamp and chairs brought from home (value $350) to decorate the office. Phone installation was $150, but he purchased a two-line telephone for $79.50.

An artist friend designed his logo and letterhead on a computer for only $25 and a $6.95 lunch. He had his stationery ($35), business cards ($60), and brochures ($23.50) produced through a local copy shop for a total of $118.50.

Since he doesn't know how to type, Bill hired his niece to work 20 hours a week for $5 per hour on an independent contractor basis so he doesn't have to pay social security or unemployment taxes.

A 2 x 2-inch display ad in the local newspaper cost him $370 for a week, so he is planning to mail 100 of his brochures to local businesses selected from the phone book. Stamps: $25 for the mailing. Office supplies, including typing paper, staples, paper clips, etc., set him back $45. A journal for record keeping cost $7.95.

He purchased a packet of invoices for $5.95 and, during the first month, has billed and been paid $700. However, he has two accounts who still owe him a total of $400. Bill dutifully records information in his cash journal at the end of each working day. He uses source documents, including his checkbook register, receipts from cash purchases and billing invoices as the basis for his entries. The two pages following are for May (prior to opening the doors of his business) and June (his first actual month in business).

Bill's expenses for May and June were $2,704.75. Of course, part of that is for start-up expenses, such as deposits on his rent and typewriter, installation costs, and one-time fictitious name filing and publishing. His income for the first month was $700.

Office Assistance
Cash Journal for May

Date	Check # Invoice #	Detail	(Debit) Expense	(Credit) Income
5/1	100	Rawlins Real Estate (Rent & dep)	$ 700.00	
5/5	101	County Clerk (Fictitious Name)	10.00	
5/7	102	The Herald (publishing FNS)	45.00	
5/9	103	Ed's Keyboards (IBM 1-mo. & dep)	275.00	
5/9	104	Ed's Keyboards (Maint. agreement)	50.00	
5/12	105	Mary Smith (Calculator purchase)	25.00	
5/18	106	Telephone company (line installation)	150.00	
5/20	107	Phone Store (2-line phone)	79.50	
5/22	108	Ray Brown (logo design)	25.00	
5/24	Cash	The Hungry Dog (lunch/Ray Brown)	6.95	
5/28	109	The Copy Spot (brochures, cards, etc.)	118.50	
5/29	110	The Herald (advertising)	370.00	
		Total Income & Expense (May)	$1,854.95	$00.00

Office Assistance
Cash Journal for June

Date	Check # Invoice #	Detail	(Debit) Expense	(Credit) Income
6/4	111	U.S.P.O (Stamps for mailing)	$ 25.00	
6/6	112	Office Stationers		
		(supplies, invoices, etc.)	58.90	
6/7	A1	W. Smith		$ 62.50
6/8	A2	Art Association		112.50
6/9	A3	T. Williams		22.00
6/9	113	Judy Miller (typing fee)	100.00	
6/10	A4	Bank of Cutterville		75.00
6/10	A5	WKTR-FM		120.50
6/13	A6	J. Johnson		43.50
6/15	114	Rawlins Real Estate (rent)	350.00	
6/15	A7	C. Lewis		73.50
6/15	A8	R. Swell		90.00
6/16	115	Judy Miller (typing fee)	100.00	
6/19	A9	W. Smith		52.50
6/23	116	Judy Miller (typing fee)	100.00	
6/26	117	Phone company (bill)	15.90	
6/27	A10	K. Black		48.00
6/30	118	Judy Miller (salary)	100.00	
		Total Income & Expense (June)	$849.80	$700.00

By deducting his expenses from his income, he can see that, at the moment, his business is showing a loss of $2,004.75.

Although Bill has only been in business for a month, he is curious about his company's financial worth and decides to work up a balance sheet to get the answer. The calculation, as indicated in the following example, is the amount owned (assets) minus the amount due to creditors (liabilities) which equals his worth.

Balance Sheet as of June 30

Assets		Liabilities	
Cash on hand & in bank	$ 7,995.25	Ed's Keyboards	$ 1,725.00
(Capital balance &		(Balance on IBM)	
June Income)		Unpaid rent (July)	350.00
Office Equipment	2,000.00	Taxes (estimated)	75.00
(includes full value			
of IBM even though			
not paid off)			
Office Furniture	350.00	Liabilities	$ 2,150.00
Accounts Receivable			
(outstanding invoices			
for work already done)	400.00		
Total Assets	$10,745.25	*CAPITAL	$ 8,595.25
		Total Liabilities	$10,745.25

The figure Bill is most interested in is the *CAPITAL amount in the Liabilities column. This is the amount remaining after what Bill owes is subtracted from his current assets and is what his business is worth at the end of June. In other words, if he decided to try and sell his business right now, he could realistically ask that amount as a sale price. Of course, Bill probably wouldn't get that amount because he has not yet become established enough to warrant someone buying the business, unless they were looking for a "turnkey" operation—

in other words, a business they could just walk into and get going immediately.

This information is valuable when Bill goes to apply for expansion capital or for credit on future purchases he plans to make, i.e., a photocopier, a computer, and new furniture. His balance sheet will change each time he prepares it (probably quarterly in the future) as business increases, bringing in more income and reducing his debts.

In the meantime, the Balance Sheet gives Bill a tool to use when comparing the financial standing of his business this month against future months and years. It also keeps him current on what he owns, to whom he owes money, and his major sources of income.

The same procedure is used in developing a personal balance sheet, which possibly would be needed to establish credibility when applying for a loan. Assets would include furniture, automobiles, jewelry, your home and other tangibles, while liabilities would consist of outstanding loans and other major debts.

Bank Statement Reconciliation

Another important step that Bill must handle monthly is reconciling his bank statement against his checkbook register. He simply marks off the checks in his register that have cleared per the statement and the deposits which have been credited, and deducts any service charges for the previous month from his balance.

Bill then adds up all the outstanding checks—those listed in his register which have not cleared by the closing date indicated on the bank statement—and *deducts* them from the balance indicated on his bank statement. He adds up any deposits which have not yet been credited to his account and then *adds* them to the balance, as follows.

Balance per bank statement	$ 7,953.44
Plus: Deposits not credited	+325.00
Minus: Outstanding checks	-115.90
New Balance	$ 8,162.54

The new balance figure should match that listed in his checkbook register and, in this case, it does. If, however, the statement and the register did not reconcile, Bill would have a customer representative at the bank review his statement and banking activity for the past month. ■

15

Pricing for Profits

One of the toughest problems facing small business owners is establishing prices that, on one hand, the market will bear while, on the other, will cover overhead and guarantee a profit.

Often new business owners give the business away to get sales, but this is not an advisable practice. Realistic pricing indicates your confidence in what you are selling and if you value your service, so will the customer.

Today's consumers realize that they can't get something worthwhile for nothing, so don't be afraid to establish prices that will work toward your profit goals.

Setting Prices for Your Newsletter

There are so many variables in producing a newsletter or a directory that it would be helpful to get advice from someone who's already published one, preferably in your vicinity. It's difficult to set a formula price, however, there are newsletters on the market that cost subscribers $20 a year for 10 issues and there are others that run an incredible $1,000 for 6 issues per year.

Part of the task of determining your price is based on the demand for the particular subject matter and your expertise in providing the information. For example, a woman in San Francisco, California, puts out an exclusive newsletter for serious investors. She gets $500 per year, based on the accuracy of her recommendations.

Bringing in Additional Income

Another factor is whether you are willing to accept advertising in your newsletter, and how much space you have to sell. Overall, however, in setting prices, you have to figure out:

1. What it's going to cost to produce the newsletter.
2. How much money you want to make.
3. How much you can charge and still be competitive.

The production method you choose can make a big difference. Printing costs can vary as much as $5,000—from 6 cents a page at a quick copy shop on plain white paper to $5 a page when you include half-toned photographs, a heavy coated stock, or color.

It's important to cover your costs, but it's especially important that you keep your costs as low as possible without, of course, compromising the quality of your product. This kind of figuring takes a certain amount of background and expertise.

Accepting Advertising

If you decide to accept advertising, it is suggested that if you do not have any experience in journalism or advertising that you find a partner who can help you set up your advertising program. Here are a few suggestions, however, to get you started:

1. To make things easier, use a format similar to a classified ad. You can charge a flat rate for, say, five lines, then add one or two extra lines for $5 per line. This format makes your layout easier. Remember that typeset material costs more, but it looks more professional.

2. You can charge an advertiser, say, $50 for a 1-column by 1-inch ad. Then, for an extra charge, you can design an ad for them. If you like, as an extra selling point, you can give your design to your advertiser to use any way they choose.
3. Offer discounts to businesses that place ads in more than one issue. For example, $50 for the first ad, $45 for the second, etc.

The benefit of accepting advertising in your newsletter is that it can actually cover all of your production costs. This means that any subscriptions you get are pure profit. The drawback to developing an advertising program is that recruiting ads is a time-consuming project. It is also possible that advertisers will inadvertantly dictate content.

Tip #2
Remember that news must be accurate, timely, and objective.

For example, if you are publishing an animal rights newsletter it would be a terrible mistake to accept advertising from, say, a cosmetic company which may perform tests on animals. Doing so would certainly affect your credibility. Of course, you always have the option of not accepting advertisers whose philosophies differ from those of the newsletter, but this could hurt your revenues if you are counting of advertising dollars to help defray expenses. These decisions are ones that must be made early on in the development of your business plan.

Price-Setting in General

Several factors must be taken into consideration when setting prices:

1. *The cost of goods sold.* In the case of a retail or wholesale operation this is the amount originally paid for the goods, while for a manufacturer it is the cost of producing the goods.
2. *The nature of the product or service.* Uniqueness and demand come into play here. In the case of goods with a stable level of demand, such as bread or auto repair, the raising or lowering of prices will have little effect. However, when demand is high for goods that are hard to get, the price can realistically be set anywhere the owner wants. Such is often the case with restaurants featuring an exclusive and unusual menu.
3. *The competition.* It is important to recognize what your competition is charging, for often this will guide pricing within a certain region. However, if a competitor is charging what you feel is an unrealistic price—either more or less—for a product or service, you owe it to yourself to find out why. Then set your prices according to all of the factors outlined here. Even if they are higher than the competitor, consumers will pay the price if you can offer an advantage, such as a friendly atmosphere, convenient hours, follow-up service or maintenance, or some other benefit not provided by the competition.
4. *Company policy.* This encompasses a number of things, including your location, your position in the marketplace, the additional services offered, and takes into account your personal philosophy about business and your role in it.
5. *Market strategy.* Should you go for large volume at low prices or for low volume at high prices? That is the bottom line in considering market strategy. As a small business owner, you will likely opt for low volume and higher prices since the alternative involves having the resources, including labor, display room, distribution channels, etc., to move large volumes of product or perform major service tasks.

6. *Customers*. What will the market bear? In other words, what are your customers willing to pay for your products or services? People expect prices that are fair; if you are planning to charge overinflated rates you had better be a top-notch salesperson or have something so incredible and unusual to offer that the price won't matter.

Although there are differences between establishing prices for retail operations, wholesale products, manufacturing and services, the basic formula for price setting is:

Labor + Materials + Overhead + Profit Margin = Price

However, before setting prices on goods or services, it is extremely important to understand the concept of the Break-Even Point. Many small business owners operate on an overall profit-loss basis without realizing the importance of cost accounting. Being aware of such factors as your break-even point, markup and profit margin can tell you which areas of your business are profitable and which are causing a drain.

Understanding Break-Even

The break-even point is the minimum amount you must charge in order to cover all expenses incurred for the production and promotion of your goods and/or services *without losing or making money*. In other words, any income which is above the break-even point is considered to be profit and anything below it is a loss.

To find your break-even point, you must first total all of your operating costs, including materials and labor, equipment lease or purchase payments, advertising, utilities, office supplies and any incidentals such as gasoline, maintenance, and postage.

Generally, this is computed for a particular period of time, such as six months or a year. However, if your business is still in the early stages of operation, you can use the estimated figures on your projected expenses statement (outlined in Chapter 7) and "guesstimated" costs for materials and labor.

For example, the monthly expenses for your hypothetical cake decorating business total $300 a month. You want to know what the break-even point would be if you sell an average of 20 cakes per month. The calculation is as follows:

$300 (expenses) ÷ 20 cakes = $15

In order to break-even, that is, to operate without losing money or realizing a profit, you must charge a minimum of $15 for each cake sold.

The same process can be used to analyze the break-even point on a weekly basis. First you would determine your annual expenses by multiplying the $300 by twelve months, which would give you $3,600 per year.

The calculation to find the weekly break-even point is:

$3,600 (expenses) ÷ 52 weeks = $69.23

Therefore, you must earn $69.23 per week to operate the business without losing money or realizing a profit.

Stay Informed

Knowing your break-even point is one of the greatest favors you can do for yourself as a business owner. It tells you how much you must charge for your products or services and is invaluable in setting prices to realize a profit.

Keep in mind, however, that the break-even point is a variable figure. Since it depends on production and overhead costs, plan to reevaluate periodically to make sure your prices reflect any changes.

Labor Costs

Labor costs, obviously, are the expenses incurred for the actual work done to manufacture or sell a product or to perform a service. Think of them as wages or salaries.

Small business owners often end up working for free because they fail to set a wage for themselves. Despite the fact that you will want to reinvest all of the income received back into the business for awhile, it is imperative that you establish a fixed salary amount for yourself when figuring operating expenses.

Money is a sixth sense
which makes it possible for us
to enjoy the other five senses.

Richard Ney

If you have set aside a survival fund to carry you through the first six months or so of operation, you may want to defer your salary until the business gets solvent, however, you should still figure the amount into your expenses. Otherwise, you may find the prices you set are too low to justify making a profit from the onset.

It is much easier to set realistic prices from the beginning than it is to raise them later in an attempt to make up the difference. Remember, your time and skills are the cornerstone of your business, so think of paying yourself as you would any valuable employee. ■

16

Inventory = Cash

Ask one hundred small business owners what inventory means to them, and more than ninety percent will tell you it's the merchandise they keep on hand to sell to their customers, or the materials and supplies stocked to produce goods or perform a service.

This is partially accurate, for inventory can and should be viewed as any supplies, raw materials, or finished goods used to generate a profit in your business. But it isn't the response that a savvy business owner would give.

Surprisingly, according to a recent study conducted by a leading consulting firm, less than ten percent of a group of five hundred entrepreneurs interviewed spoke of their inventory in terms of the *investment it represents*; an investment that can range from fifteen to twenty-five percent of total operating capital.

It is because of this "misunderstanding" that many small business owners often fail to incorporate good inventory control practices into their regular management routine. Although they keep an eagle eye on every penny going through the books, they may totally overlook the cash tied up in their inventory.

As the Business Grows

Inventory control can be a very simple, straightforward task if you implement a workable system from the beginning — preferably even *before* you start ordering and receiving goods.

You will find that time really flies when you are self-employed and it's easy to postpone such tasks as inventory control until, the inevitable day you find yourself facing this overwhelming job.

Inventory control will give you valuable information about:

1. Whether or not you are carrying too much or too little inventory based on, for example, items and prices preferred by your customers, or seasonal aspects, and
2. Whether you are realizing optimum economy determined by the costs of storage, taxes, handling, and the investment per unit.

The ideal situation is to maintain an inventory that is profitable because it turns over (comes in and goes out of the business) regularly, thereby lowering the cost of storing, displaying, and insuring it.

---

*Although there are countless alumni
of the school of hard knocks,
there has not yet been a move
to accredit that institution.*

Sonya Rudikoff

There are several methods of inventory control that you can adopt, depending on your business. The main goal with each method, however, is to tell you how many items you have on hand and how many you need to meet your customer or production demands. It will also work toward lessening inventory shrinkage, which is generally the result of employee pilferage, customer theft, storing inventory incorrectly, or maintaining sloppy records of items ordered, received, and used.

You can tell how many items you currently have by making an educated guess, which generally only works for businesses having a small, visible inventory that is relatively predictable. An example of the kind the business which could probably operate efficiently with this 'relaxed' form of inventory control would be a one-person cleaning service which weekly goes through, say, a bottle of window cleaner and similar supplies available for a minimum amount at the local supermarket.

Other methods of inventory control are *the physical count*, which should be done at least once a year anyway for tax purposes, or—the easiest and most efficient of them all—*maintaining an ongoing record*. The best idea is to incorporate both systems; to back up periodic physical counts with a perpetual record.

To set up your perpetual system, simply create a file card or inventory sheet in a three-ring binder for each item in your inventory. Across the top of the card or sheet, list the following:

1. Item name and a code number (if applicable).
2. A description of the item.
3. Where it is stored.
4. The supplier's name, address, and phone number.
5. Unit price (e.g., $12.95/dozen).
6. Your selling price if a retail item, or percentage of gross price of completed product, if used for manufacturing or service.
7. The date you place an order.
8. The number of items and the date they are received.

Then, every time you sell or use an item, write it down and subtract it from the last balance. You should also indicate reorder number, based on when and by how much you must replenish your stock.

The reorder number will be determined by such factors as:

1. The minimum cost per unit available from your supplier, including quantity discounts, preseason specials and discounts for cash or quick payment.
2. The delivery schedule, the delay between placing the order and receiving it.
3. Economic and social trends which can affect the way an item is perceived by the public.

For example, during a period of depressed or inflated economy, sales for leisure items typically drop. By keeping an eye on these factors, you can adjust your inventory needs accordingly and not get stuck with great quantities of items that you can't move.

After a while, you will be able to recognize at-a-glance which items are movers and which are simply taking up shelf space. When you reach this point, your ordering skills will become much more efficient and your investment in inventory will become a profitable proposition. ▪

17

Getting Down to Business

A recent survey of small business owners indicated that one of the qualities they felt contributed the most to their success was organization. In conjunction with this is the fact that time management and basic organizational seminars continue to be the most popular offerings in adult education catalogs and business workshops around the country.

Time is money! Because the small business owner is plagued by a unique set of problems, such as continual interruptions and overworking, it is vital to your success that you learn to manage your time and organize paperwork. This might sound rather simplistic, but you would be amazed at the number of small business owners who operate in a constant state of chaos.

Although we have seen a number of "A messy office is the sign of a creative mind" posters on entrepreneur's office walls, it is a good bet that the holders of these signs can recount story after story of missing checks, lost orders and misplaced files that totally disrupted the flow of business until they were located in a corner pile.

The survey respondents also stated that once they had learned to manage their time in both their personal and business lives and had set up guidelines for handling routine tasks, they felt more confident about accepting new challenges and making decisions.

The simple truth about getting organized is that it clears your mind for the taking care of the nitty-gritty, profit-making aspects of being in business—production and promotion. For example, just by allotting a certain place in your desk to hold customer files and billing information, you have made one major step towards maximizing production. Knowing that all the supplies and materials needed to conduct your business are located in one spot saves valuable time when you have a job to get out.

Time Tools

Time management is the ability to take the hours we have available and use them to our advantage. Making lists of tasks to be done and giving them a priority rating, as outlined above, is one of the best ways to avoid losing precious moments.

Keep a monthly calendar handy to help you keep track of major commitments, important dates and appointments. Try to avoid using it for notations of daily work in progress, carry-over tasks or other things that are best suited for inclusion on your daily and weekly lists.

There are several other ideas you can easily incorporate into your working lifestyle that will maximize your productivity.

Work smart. Handle the jobs you find most difficult or cumbersome during peak performance time. If you are a morning person and find that making telephone calls to potential customers is one of your least favorite responsibilities, take care of them first thing in the morning when you are feeling fresh and energetic, and organize the rest of the day's tasks accordingly.

Set realistic daily goals for yourself. Just because you are chief cook and bottlewasher, don't try to do everything at once. Learn just how much work you can accept and expect to accomplish in a given period of time and allow yourself to turn down work if it seems like it will be too much for you to handle.

Reward yourself. When you are working alone, as many small business owners do when getting their businesses off the ground, there generally aren't many people anywhere around to support or praise your work... and everyone needs strokes! While it is true that a customer's praises are an indication that you are doing the right thing, you still need time to relax.

Treat yourself to a special dinner once a week. If money is especially tight, plan an evening where you go to bed early with a good book or do something that has absolutely nothing to do with business. And remind yourself that this is your reward for accomplishing certain goals for the week. It will help to keep your spirits high.

Don't procrastinate. Don't put off doing tasks that must be done. If you constantly let some tasks slide because you don't enjoy doing them, you will soon find yourself terribly back-logged and unable to catch up. The effects of this may not show themselves until you are faced with a deadline and, at that point, you will discover that you are working at less than maximum efficiency, feeling tense and being hassled by small things. Even when business is slow and it seems that there could be little harm done by taking a day off to visit with a friend, be sure to complete required tasks before closing up shop.

Limit personal phone calls during established business hours. Personal calls not only eat into productive time, they tie up the line when an important client may be trying to get in touch with you. The same holds true with friendly visitations. If you are self-employed, friends often feel that you are not really 'working' and can stop anytime to chat. Explain that you will be happy to visit with them at a specific time and be sure to tell them why so there aren't any ruffled feathers.

Obviously, there will be times when unavoidable situations, such as an emergency or an unexpected problem, arise.

Try to take these inevitabilities into consideration by estimating how long a project will take and then adding a bit of extra time to give yourself leeway.

Delegate. If you find that you absolutely cannot handle a certain aspect of the business, such as your own bookkeeping, for example, don't labor over the task—you will end up wasting a great deal of time and could make some serious mistakes. Admit to yourself that the task is just not a strong point and make arrangements to have someone else do it.

Learn to say "No." One of the hardest things for most people to do is to say "no." Even when we realize that, for example, helping a friend out on a special project will eat into valuable time, we often agree to do such things because we hate to say no. What we do is justify our acceptance by assuring ourselves that saying yes will put us in the position of meeting a lot of potential customers. The reality is that using that time to make phone calls or a sales call for your own business will probably result in a paying customer, not just a potential contact.

Minimize business meetings. Before setting up a formal meeting, which can be very time-consuming, see if you can take care of the matter in question by phone or through the mail. If a meeting can't be avoided, make sure you specify a time limit to encourage people to get down to business. Another time-saving device for meetings is to work up an agenda that outlines exactly what has to be discussed to avoid idle chit-chat and unnecessary diversions. ■

18

Producing Your Newsletter

Content

Without good content, design means nothing. Your readers assume that you have access to information they can't easily get for themselves. They believe you will help them understand what the news means. The meaning of your news is at least as important as its subject matter.

The more you advise, interpret and analyze, the more useful your newsletter becomes. You are not obliged to tell your readers everything you have heard, but you do owe them your insight as well as up-to-date information.

Story Ideas

How do you deliver the information your readers want? There are several ways. You can have a column that interviews experts in your field—authors, teachers, consultants, executives, speakers. The list goes on and on. Interviews are generally informative and fun to read because they involve a personality. Competitions and awards are newsworthy. You can talk about who won what, and how these competitions affect quality and productivity.

Articles can also deal with the following issues as they relate to your area of specialization:

- Bottom line goals and values
- Cutting costs

- Where to find certain services
- Growth of the industry overall
- New technology
- Specific trade or professional organizations
- Profiles of members
- Resources and suppliers
- Taxes
- Training
- Trends
- Efficient ways to work

To keep tabs on current information, you will want to keep a list of key names and phone numbers in your file to make your rounds of calls before each deadline. You will want to get yourself on mailing lists for important releases and reports, as well as other newsletters.

It is not enough to have great qualities,
we should also have management of them.

La Rochefoucauld

Keeping an idea file is a necessity for newsletter editors. You never know when old notes, clippings, or references will save your day by offering you something to put in that space you have absolutely no information for. Be sure to let everyone know that you need information and help to make your newsletter visible.

You may have a column in your newsletter encouraging customer letters to either voice opinions or ask for specific information. This is one way of staying in touch with client need.

Copyright

If you want to reproduce copyrighted material, or prevent your own material from being reproduced without permission, you need to be aware of the copyright law. You cannot copyright the name of your newsletter, but you can copyright the graphic rendition of that name (your logo).

If you are preparing to use material written and published by someone else, look for the phrase "Copyright (date plus name of owner)." The symbol "©" may appear instead of the word "copyright."

What Do Readers Like?

Of course, every newsletter must include certain kinds of information to satisfy the readership. Here is a list of ideas for regular columns you may wish to incorporate:

Anecdotes	*Classified Ads*
Calendar of Events	*Letters to the Editor*
Personality Profiles	*Q & A Column*
Industry News	*Motivational Material*
Hobby News	*Suggestions*
Trends and Changes	*Potpourri of Quotes*
Book Reviews	*Seminar Programs*
Guest Columnists	*Topic Jargon*
How-To Information	*Reports from Special*
History of the Subject	*Interest Groups*

Public Domain

Any articles, drawings or photographs whose copyrights have expired can be used without permission. These are said to be in the public domain. If you want, however, to use copyrighted material in your newsletter, you must either acquire the owner's permission or publish under the provisions of fair use.

You can write to the copyright owner for permission, sending a sample of your newsletter and a self-addressed, stamped envelope for a reply. You should indicate that you will publish whatever credit line the copyright owner desires. If your newsletter is for commercial gain, you may be asked to pay a fee for the right.

Fair use refers to reproducing portions of copyrighted material without permission for the purpose of teaching, analysis, or review. It is a good idea to always give due credit when doing this. Fair use means you have not deprived the copyright owner of profit.

Protecting *Your* Work

If you write or draw something you do not want to be duplicated, you should copyright it for protection. The easiest way to protect yourself is to put the copyright phrase in the masthead of your newsletter. For specific copyright information and registration, write to the Copyright Office, Library of Congress, Washington, DC 20559.

If your newsletter advocates a cause or promotes public relations, you might be very happy to have your material reproduced. These newsletters should not be copyrighted and should specify in their mastheads that permission is granted to reproduce, provided that appropriate credit is given to the original publication.

Copyright law can get pretty technical. If you have any doubts, it would be advisable to consult some copyright books or an attorney who is informed of copyright law.

Define Your Purpose

1. Who is the audience?
2. Why do they need the newsletter?
3. Is your intention to report the facts, analyze material or provide motivation?
4. What would your readers prefer?
5. Do you have the time and resources to produce the kind of newsletter you and the readers want?

Writing

Good writing comes from re-writing—always go over your work repeatedly to ensure clarity and readability. Writing can be a pleasure, but it is hard work and requires proper time and conditions. You need at least two to three hours in a row and you need to work without distractions or interruptions.

Writing Eye-Catching Headlines

Newspapers and magazines generally write headlines after re-reading articles. It is advisable for newsletter writers to write their headlines first. This helps you focus on what your article will say. It will help you determine how important the article is with regard to other articles in the issue. Headlines attract attention to your article, so you want them to pull your readers in.

Bad: "Songwriter Update"
Good: "Leslie Lompoc Gets Song Recorded on RCA"

Headlines should have a verb and be in the present tense. All news worth its salt is in the present. A headline should tell as much of your story as possible. A specific headline tends to be active, not passive, and gets your subject matter noticed.

Write It Like You Say It

Writing style should be informal and natural; conversational in tone. You have a small amount of space to offer a great amount of information. You want the newsletter's personality to show and its information to be easily understood. Good writing is simple, specific, compact, active, strong, and fun to read.

All writing can be improved by copyediting and proof-reading. If you are not adept at either of these tasks, you might want to consider hiring someone to make sure that your words are spelled properly and stated clearly. An experienced editor can make your important information sound alive and easy to understand.

Format

Format consists of the components you decide to use for your newsletter, consistent with its goals, objectives, and readership. It includes page size, number of columns of type, and the dimensions of each column. Format is the framework of your publication. The best and most pleasing to the eye is usually the most simple.

It's advisable to put your format on paper, even if it exists in computer memory. Make a dummy setup that shows column widths, margins and borders. A representation on paper shows you precisely how it looks. Format helps ensure accurate work. It tells you how much space a story and its headline might require.

Standard newsletter size is 8-1/2" x 11" with the page broken up into one, two or three columns. Before deciding on your format, you might want to make several mockups to see how your information is best presented.

Typography

Typeface is the most important element of design. Badly selected type can make your content difficult to read. Although sometimes confusing, decisions about type for a newsletter need to be made probably only once every two or three years.

There are four sources of type for body copy and headlines. There are others that are appropriate only for headlines.

Strike-on type. This is the kind made by typewriters and computer printers with print wheels, with one stroke of a key, ball or daisy wheel. Their output is generally termed "letter quality." Cloth ribbons make for fuzzy type because the weave of the cloth is uneven.

Dot matrix type. Many computer printers use this method of pin points hitting a ribbon to form characters. Most are adjustable to two or three densities, one of which is near-letter quality. The type is often fuzzy and hard to read.

Laser type. Laser printers form characters when toner, a special powder, sticks to dots on paper charged by a pulsating laser beam. Dots from a laser printer are larger than those from a dot matrix printer and are printed at a fairly tight density. The type they create is excellent for most newsletters. If you can afford a laser printer (in the area of $5,000), that's the one to buy.

If not, there are computer shops that will allow you to bring
your disk in to print on their laser printer for a small fee.

Photo type.   This is the highest quality type and comes from
machines that use laser beams to form characters on photo-
sensitive paper. The paper is smoother and whiter and the dots
are much smaller than can be produced with either toner or
pins.

Proofreading Tips

1.   If possible, have someone else proofread your copy. It is
     especially difficult to watch for spelling errors, grammar,
     and content, when it is your own material that you've been
     working with for hours or maybe days.
2.   If you must do your own proofreading, read everything
     through the first time in blocks, such as all the body copy,
     all the headlines and then all the captions, to catch obvious
     errors. Then proofread everything word for word, but
     backwards (or right to left across each line) to check for
     spelling. The third time through, check for capitals and
     punctuation. And then, read for content. Make sure all
     major thoughts are completed and that copy is written in
     the desired tone.
3.   Be sure to double check the spelling of names, dates, times
     of events, phone numbers, and other pertinent facts.

Choosing Typefaces

There are more than 5,000 typefaces in existence today. A first
rate newsletter can be produced, however, by working with

only one or two. Familiar typefaces promote easy reading. New or unusual designs will often detract from content. Unless you have some experience as a graphic designer, choose type such as Times or Helvetica, which have a proven record.

Typography, graphics, and photography are all important to know if you are about to embark on a newsletter venture. Classes are taught in most colleges and even in some adult education or community center courses. Each area has its own special language to learn, and as you go you will become more familiar with them.

Type is either plain, **bold**, *italics,* or <u>underscored.</u> Styles of type are numerous, and knowing how to combine them for easy and effective reading is an art that you can develop by examining magazines and graphics books and then applying techniques that attract attention to your newsletter design.

Incorporating Artwork

Graphics consist of lines or rules, screen tints, reverses, illustrations, and diagrams. *Rules* are borders and boxes, and are among the easiest graphics to produce. *Screen tints* are shadings or patterns that look like light versions of the ink or toner. They are used to highlight blocks of type, such as mastheads and tables of contents. *Reverses* are images made by printing the background rather than the image itself. Black becomes white, and white becomes black.

Illustrations consist of drawings and technical illustrations, as well as "clip art," which are generic drawings made specifically to sell to designers, printers, and others needing instant graphics. Drawings are often copyrighted, so you want to remember to check before using them.

Diagrams generally consist of charts, graphs, tables, and maps. They are powerful newsletter tools because they carry so much information in so little space. A good way to test every chart or graph is to show it to someone unfamiliar with the information you want to get across. If you have to explain what the diagram means, it isn't working.

Dealing with Photographs

The best photo advice we have heard from newsletter editors is to overexpose and underdevelop black and white film. If you use 400 ASA film, set your camera at 200, and tell the darkroom to cut development time by twenty-five percent. Other than this, think about the kind of photo you want for a particular story and be sure that it enhances the story as well as your newsletter. Photographs add to your printing costs and to your work time, so be sure that you want them. Photos convey feelings rather than words, so use them to capture the essence of a particular moment.

Design and Layout

Good design and layout ensure clear, enjoyable reading. Newsletter design includes format, type specifications, and the ordering of such elements as the nameplate. Layout is the way the design is carried out for a specific issue.

The primary purpose of design is to make the content accessible. Design can stimulate a reader's interest and make reading efficient, but it cannot hide poor content or careless writing. The items to pay close attention to in design are: Nameplate, color, masthead, calendar, layout, and photo layout.

The nameplate is at the top of the front page, because is what readers see first and foremost. The design and information influence how readers perceive your newsletter. Pick a good one and stay with it.

When used well, color creates contrast and makes certain elements more vivid. A second color can be used at little extra cost by using the technique of pre-printing—which means having color printed on enough paper at one time to last for many issues. This means a certain portion of your masthead, for example, could be done in a second color.

Specifics such as the date could not be preprinted, since that is a variable. It is best to consult with a graphic designer if you plan to use more than one color, because color influences feelings and some colors reproduce better than others. Consult a professional to make sure you choose the right colors for your newsletter.

A table of contents is advisable for newsletters longer than eight pages, and sometimes helpful for those of only four pages. It functions as an advertisement for the information inside and often adds to the design of your front page.

Calendars do not need to be complicated or fancy—only well-organized and complete. A helpful calendar will be full of information and anticipate questions:

> April 12-14
> Anytown, USA
> Songwriter Workshop.

This is the "basic" workshop for new or relatively experienced songwriters, but is also valuable for the longtime professional seeking new ideas.

Good layout is a matter of knowing what articles and graphics you want in an issue and how important each one is. Some elements will appear earlier; some will be longer; some will be larger. Priority tells you what gets the largest headline, and what gets bumped into the pile called "stuff for other issues." It's always advisable to make up a dummy sheet indicating what will go where, so you can see it in time to change it if it doesn't work visually. Successful layouts are simple, well structured, allow the reader's eye to flow, and are well proportioned.

Odds Versus Evens

Photo layouts generally work better in odd numbers—three or five instead of two or four. It's best to arrange the images flowing left to right or top to bottom, the way that we read. All photo images should be of the same quality. One bad one will make everything look bad. The most dynamic photo spreads have plenty of surrounding space, so don't be afraid to leave white space. Uneven margins are best.

Don't forget that photos in spreads need captions, so leave room for them. You will need to anticipate where the crease falls, since most photo spreads run across folds. You don't want someone's face underneath the staple. Photo layouts generally require a pasteup, so leave yourself time for doing this.

Ready for the Printer

Once your layout is prepared, you will be ready for printing. Newsletters are printed either on offset presses or photocopy machines. Whichever method you use, paper is a major cost. Whether a commercial or a quick offset printer is best for your newsletter depends on your needs for quality, quantity, and service. Commercial printers produce higher quality than quick printers.

How much quality you need depends on your particular market. Quick print presses use paper or plastic plates, as opposed to metal ones. Quick copy printers are your best bet for press runs up to about 2,000 copies. After 2,000, a quick printer's price is not likely to be lower than a traditional offset print shop. Whichever printer you choose, remember that good customers get good service. Make sure the copy you are delivering is clean and complete, and that you get your materials to the printer when you say you will.

Ask for a Proof

A proof is a test sheet, made to show errors or flaws and record how your newsletter is supposed to appear, before it's actually printed. Every issue of your newsletter should be proofed before going to press. It is the only way to be certain that your mechanicals, negatives, and plates are accurate and complete. Proofs also help determine who is responsible for mistakes and should pay for corrections.

Tip #3

*Use art to make a statement about
the copy in your newsletter.*

When you inspect your proofs, keep in mind individual features, photos and drawings, flaws, previous corrections, instructions, finishing, colors, questions, and costs. Circle every blemish, and ask about anything that seems wrong. This is your last chance to make everything look perfect.

Whether you pay on delivery, invoice or statement, check everything in your printing job before authorizing payment. If you question an invoice, discuss the matter candidly. You can ensure a good relationship with your printer by being reasonable and understanding the printer's point of view. Say, "Thanks. Nice job," when you really think so.

Keep in mind that the cost of paper represents twenty percent to fourty percent of your newsletter printing cost. Upgrading your paper stock is an easy and inexpensive way to improve the appearance of the newsletter. Money spent on raising paper quality, however, might be better spent on a professional design or computer software, or even computer training.

Distribution and Mail Matters

Most newsletters reach readers by mail. Before starting your newsletter, pick up a set of postal regulations from the local post office and read them to find cost-saving opportunities. If you find postal regulations difficult to wade through, contact a Pitney Bowes Corporation distributor in your city for information and easy-to-follow handbooks.

Address lists. You can save money by ensuring that your newsletter goes only to people who want it, that their addresses are correct, and that you presort each mailing. When you consider what you pay to print, fold, and address your newsletters, you don't want to send a substantial number to people who perhaps are not interested in the subject matter. Study your address list on a periodic basis and make sure each name belongs. If people have not renewed their subscription, do not continue to send them copies of the newsletter.

If you have a computer, create an address list and make sure all names are in a database or mailing program that can be sorted by zip code. The database programs should have seperate fields, such as renewal dates, which you can use to monitor your mailing.

Address labels. Postal regulations dictate size, color, return address, and zip codes, as well as location and format of addresses. Find out what they are and how they apply in your town.

Mail classifications.   Commercial newsletter publishers use first class mail to convey an image of importance. Even organizations with small budgets sometimes use first class mail to be sure that news of special events arrives in a timely manner. First class postage is determined by the ounce; the weight of your paper affects what you pay. Check the weight of papers before you commit to a stock so that there are no unanticipated expenses when the time comes to do the mailing.

First class mail will be returned if not deliverable, so you can clean up your mailing list. This winds up being cheaper and less troublesome in the long run than doing a subscriber check.

Newsletters sent at least four times a year may be mailed second class. Second class pieces receive the same handling as first class, but rates are much lower. Costs are based on account percentages of advertising and editorial content, as well as weight and other minor factors. If you want first class service for about half the cost, do what it takes to get your newsletter classified for second class.

Third class is bulk rate.   It is the least expensive mail category. Rates are generally half of first class. Each piece of third class mail must be identical, except for the address, and all pieces must be presorted before being brought to the post office. There is a 200 piece minimum. Third class mail takes longer. If you use it, mail in the middle of the month to avoid competing with large first class mailings and in the middle of the week to avoid the deluge of second class magazines and newspapers.

Non-profit status.   Organizations that are not for profit can send second and third class mail for about half of what commercial mailers pay. Only certain groups qualify for this status, however. Apply to the United States Postal Service for this rate if you have qualified for non-profit status with the government.

Pre-sorting. In the case of first class mail, presorting is optional and gets you a twenty percent discount. You must send at least 500 newsletters and you get a slightly higher discount for using ZIP + 4 codes. In second and third class mail, presorting is required.

Presorting is worthwhile for large mailings. If you send, for example, 40,000 copies of a monthly newsletter, presorting may save you $2,400 per year in postage. If you lack only a few names to make the minimum for a 200 or 500 presort, you will save money if you add your name and perhaps those of a few friends to the mailing list to make the minimum number.

Presorting does involve some costs. There is a small annual permit fee. Also, someone must do the presorting other than the post office. Decide if it is cost efficient for you to be performing this task.

Mailing services. Preparing several thousand newsletters for mailing is tedious and complex, and it often makes sense to let a mailing service handle the job. Mailing services, or letter-shops, specialize in large mailings and know how to do them right. They have machines to put glue on labels and affix them to your newsletter. They have personnel trained to presort and get them sacked according to post office regulations. Most mailing services have computers and high-speed printers to help you maintain your mailing list.

Look under "mailing services" in the phone directory to find services in your area. Some communities have workshops run by organizations like Goodwill and United Cerebral Palsy whose workers label, sort, and bundle newsletters. They take longer, but charge less.

The Newsletter and Beyond

When your renewals begin to arrive regularly, and your overhead is small, you can use your newsletter as a base to spin off other publications, books, or seminars. Every subscriber becomes a resource to tap—a proven customer willing to write a check in exchange for valuable facts, figures, or insights. Supplementary books or workshops may draw on information you have already gathered for your newsletter. Therefore, even modest sales can turn wonderful profits.

Producing a successful newsletter on schedule and within budget is an accomplishment. There are more newsletters than ever doing well in the marketplace. Computer technology is making them easier than ever to create.

Choosing Your Newsletter

The best situation for a newsletter requires careful thought. You need to know what results your readership wants from your publication. Basically, however, newsletters work well when the information provided is portable and inexpensive. Successful newsletters have an audience composed of people with a common interest, and that common interest should be specific. A "How To Raise Dogs" newsletter will not work as well as one that focuses on "How to Raise Cocker Spaniels". Good newsletters do not compete with books, movies, or TV. They contain precise information that readers can use. Both the reader and the sponsor see the newsletter as a service.

Successful newsletters are personal. The editor becomes a household name—someone who can be called on the phone with a question or comment or written to directly. The news is short, to the point and can be absorbed very quickly; and it relates to the recent past, the present or the immediate future. This, of course, means that issues of the publication must come out often enough to assure that each one is current.

The Purpose of Your Newsletter

Are you marketing something? An idea? A product? A service? Marketing newsletters raise money, increase organization membership, influence votes, or promote greater patronage of a particular facility. This type of newsletter focuses on action.

Newsletters for public relations focus on attitudes rather than actions. Good public relations will make readers more receptive to marketing or to the goals of a particular organization. The best ones capture the attention of readers who may otherwise lack interest in the topics reported. They build respect for content, support for causes, and good will for sponsors.

Publications for internal relations are those read by employees or members. They honor outstanding performances, build morale, and stimulate attention to quality. The best internal newsletters are not strictly the voice of management, but those that help shape organizational vision and promote a feeling of togetherness among all employees.

Commercial newsletters, the kind you are most interested in working on, can be any of the above newsletters. Newsletters for profit make money for you and provide solid information. Sometimes newsletters for profit go to organizations that redistribute them to employees or clients. Sometimes buyers will imprint their own name on a newsletter when distributing them, to make it appear that their own product is being sold. You may have seen publications of this kind from insurance agents or medical clinics.

Defining Your Goals

You would be wise to write down the goals of your newsletter and then narrow them down to no more than four or five. Do you want to advise your readers of something? Analyze certain information? Announce new findings? Assure the reader or evaluate certain statistics? Do you want to guide, honor, illustrate, influence, inform, inspire, persuade, praise, or support? Use these words when starting to define your goals.

Establish Your Objectives

Your objectives are basically geared to the end results for your readership. Goals may define your direction, but objectives deal with what actually is, or will be, your destination. Why is your newsletter worth the time and money required to produce it?

Helpful objectives describe how those who read it will be better off. The perfect objective describes a result that can be measured. For instance, how many dollars will be saved, or the date on which a project will be completed. Writing strong objectives may require some time and re-writing. For example:

Goal. Contribute to the success of songwriters (a general direction).

Objective. Help songwriters who are trying to publish songs to be more effective (a specific result to be achieved).

Better objective. Help songwriters learn to be efficient in their song pitches so both they and their prospective publishers spend less time making more money. Specific objectives make you ask if a newsletter is a practical way to accomplish this goal with this audience. If you stop meeting your goals, it's all over.

Determining Quality

Budget is not the only factor in whether or not your newsletter will be a success; design and writing are equally important.

Time, skill, and care will make a big difference. The design of your nameplate alone will heavily influence your readership's perception of the quality of your newsletter.

You also want the newsletter to take on its own personality. Is it neighborly or authoritative? Are you acting as an objective observer or an enthusiastic insider? Are you going to be an intimate advisor or a detached bystander?

Administrative Decisions

Length.   Most newsletters are either two pages (one sheet 8-1/2" x 11"), four pages (one sheet 11" x 13"), or eight pages (twenty sheets 11"x 17"). These lengths and sizes are standards; they can be produced inexpensively.

Frequency.   Four times a year is probably a minimum. Monthly is the most common. A shorter newsletter arriving more frequently works better than a longer publication arriving less often. More issues means higher distribution costs and more deadlines, but meeting each deadline requires less time writing and producing.

Timing.   Readers should have the newsletter in front of them at least a week before the first date on the calendar of future events. Such timing will determine your deadlines. When setting a schedule, you will want to work backward from when you know you want copies in your readers' hands. Be careful estimating distribution speed. It is often delayed.

Schedule.   Write yourself a production schedule for each newsletter; perhaps there is a form you can make up and photocopy for each deadline schedule. Write in the date each production step must be completed by. This would include such categories as Select Topics for Issue, Write Material,

Typesetting, Get Artwork, Special Design Tasks, Proofing, Printing, Shipping, and Prepare for Mailing. Live by those dates.

Quantity. Print more copies than you have subscriptions for, because you should definitely have extra copies to give away for promotional purposes. In addition, new subscribers may want back issues. Printing an extra ten percent to fifteen percent adds little to your production costs. ■

19

Hiring Employees

One of the benefits of starting small is that you don't have to hire anyone to work for you. As the business grows and your subscriptions increase or you decide to start a second newsletter, however, you will probably want to have some help, at least on an as-needed basis.

Unless business is booming, don't worry about hiring anyone other than free-lancers. You can find reliable free-lance writers and/or graphics designers familiar with newsletter publishing through various means: ads in the paper, lists at local computer stores, cards on bulletin boards, and so on. Whenever you see someone advertising his or her services, take down the name and number. Because free-lancing in any field is often a "feast or famine" business, most of the people you contact will be happy for the extra work.

Knowledge is of two kinds. We know a subject ourselves or we know where we can find information on it.

Samuel Johnson

If you decide you'd rather have someone on a regular salary, you get into an entirely different area of business management. Now you are an *employer*, and there are certain re-

sponsibilities you have that might make free-lancers seem all
the more attractive.

The bottom line is this: You want to make money with this
business. Until you have the volume to justify a staff, keep all
your help free-lance. You will not only save money, but you
will develop a list of dependable workers you can call on again
and again.

In terms of what you should pay your workers, you'll find
that most free-lancers come with standard fee that is often
flexible (because most free-lancers live hand-to-mouth and are
always looking for work). Check around and see what a reasonable rate of pay is, and pay accordingly.

An important note: Don't try to pay less than a free-lancer
is worth, because you'll often get work that is commensurate.
By the same token, don't accept sub-standard work from
someone who's being paid to do a quality job.

But both of these problems can be overcome if you apply
the following guidelines:

- *Recruit on a consistent basis.* Even if you are fully staffed,
  interview potential employees regularly so you have
  names to draw on in the event that someone quits suddenly
  or is unable to show up for any reason. Men and women are
  equally suited for employment in your business.
- *Create a sense of team spirit.* Let your employees know
  they are vital to the success of the business. Although you
  can't afford to be "friends" with everyone, do let them
  know you are available for moral support and compas-
  sionate about their feelings. Some owners hold monthly
  meetings so that employees can share their experiences on
  the job and talk about ways to handle clients or problems
  they encounter on the road more effectively. Communication is a necessary factor in successful employee relations
  because the business is so personal.

• *Be flexible.* The majority of your workers will probably have family responsibilities. If you are willing to arrange work schedules around individual needs, your employees will be appreciative and more likely to make an effort to please you and the clients.

As soon as you feel you are ready, place an ad in the classified ads of the local newspaper to recruit potential workers. Also register with your State Unemployment office. Students, who will only be available on a seasonal basis but are generally good workers, can be found by contacting placement offices at major colleges and universities. In addition, you can often find excellent candidates in friends or family members of current employees.

Selection of Candidates

Be prepared to go through quite a few people who are just looking for interim employment or who simply do not present a good image before you find a few good candidates willing to make a commitment to the job. If at all possible, you want to avoid spending time training people who are not going to stay with the company.

The Interview Process

Schedule a personal interview to make your own determination based on poise, appearance, level of interest in the job, abilities and future goals. Write out any questions you may have ahead of time to help you stay on track.

Set up the interview in a comfortable place to put the candidate at ease. For example, if you operate out of your home, you may want to arrange to meet in a convenient restaurant during a slow time or if you have an office, set it up when you won't be bombarded by phone calls or people stopping in.

In addition to finding out about their capabilities and goals, you will want to use this time to talk about the company, your expectations, standards and, of course, the pay structure.

Training Your Techniques

When you find someone who seems to have all the qualifications needed, arrange to train them on-the-job. Many owners like to do this themselves, to ensure that their standards are instilled from the beginning and to get a first-hand idea of the new recruit's work habits. But if you have a trusted employee on staff, have the new recruit accompany them on assignments to learn the ropes. . . this extra duty should always result in a bonus for the employee doing the training.

Training your techniques may take several weeks or months, depending on the worker's previous experience. Basically, a good training process should involve the following steps:

1. Gain the recruit's confidence by putting him or her at ease.
2. Find out what he or she already knows.
3. Indicate the importance of the specific task being taught.
4. Explain and show each step patiently.
5. Be sure each step is understood before moving on to another.
6. Encourage and welcome questions.
7. Have the recruit try to do the task.
8. Correct mistakes gently.
9. Have him or her repeat the steps to you.
10. When you are both comfortable, let the recruit go out alone.
11. Review performance periodically.

12. Offer support by letting the employee train others when ready.

Taking time to train properly reduces turnover and accidents, improves the quality of work performed and lowers your cost of labor.

The Benefits of Happy Employees

Personnel management is a time-consuming job for business owners. However, paying attention to the needs of your employees and working to gain their trust and maintain loyalty can do nothing but benefit your business.

The attitude of your employees about your management techniques plays an important part in building and maintaining your reputation in the business world. If employees are treated fairly and with respect, their job satisfaction will be reflected in the way they do their job.

This is something that can truly keep you ahead of the competition; a loyal, efficient and enthusiastic group of workers is one of your most effective forms of public relations, so never scrimp when it comes to keeping your employees happy. A few important rules of thumb in dealing with employees include the following:

- *Never expect an employee to do something that you wouldn't do.* This is why training new recruits yourself is such a good idea; it shows them that you are willing and able to step in and do anything required if necessary.
- *Listen to your employees* and incorporate their ideas whenever it is feasible. They have first-hand knowledge about how certain aspects of the job can be done more efficiently. Suggestions that work for the good of the company should be rewarded with a bonus.

- *Take the time to talk about business standards* and practices so that everyone knows exactly what is expected of them. Outline duties and responsibilities on the job and schedule regular reviews to ensure that they are constantly met. If you find it necessary to talk to an employee about their work habits, do it in private so they are not embarrassed in front of their peers. And do not criticize; merely offer constructive ways that they can improve their performance.
- *Treat each employee as an individual.* When someone seems to be having personal problems that are interfering with their ability to work, be willing to allow them time off without penalty to take care of the situation. An employee plagued with problems may carry them to work and this could have a negative effect. It is much better to get someone to fill in until the regular employee is operating at full efficiency again. ■

20

Advertising Your Business

More than 150 years ago, Thomas Macaulay, a British historian and statesman, said, "Advertising is to business what steam is to industry. [They provide] the same propelling power."

Few in business would argue with Macaulay's observation—it is as true today as it was when steam was the driving force behind industry. But the question remains, "How do you get the most out of your advertising dollar?" The answer is to:

1. Know your customer,
2. Target your market, and
3. Understand the basics of advertising.

In this chapter, we will provide an overview of various aspects of advertising, including how to use circulation figures to figure your Cost Per Thousand (CPM) and how to create ads that will bring results.

What is Advertising?

Advertising informs the public about:

- Who you are,
- What kind of business you operate,
- How they can buy your products or services, and
- Why they should come to you.

Before you even open the doors of your business, you should start thinking about your advertising program—how much money you can afford to spend, where your dollars will be best spent, and how to structure your campaign.

Decide what kind of results you expect. Are you looking for immediate sales or ongoing recognition? What kind of customers are you hoping to attract? Are you emphasizing price, service, workmanship or something unique? Once you have answered these questions, your decision as to the best type of advertising for the allotted dollars will be easier to make.

There are three basic types of advertising that you will be most interested in during the first few years of your business.

Start-up advertising. This includes your business cards and stationery, the flyers and brochures you have created to pass out around the neighborhood announcing your new business, and your initial newspaper advertising campaign. At this point, your main focus will be on telling people where you are located and what you can offer them.

Ongoing advertising. Once the business is "up and running," so to speak, it will be vital to your success to institute a regular advertising campaign that is well planned and—this is the key—consistent. Your goal, at this point, is to maintain your established customers, increase your market base, introduce new products or services and promote sales to clear inventory, or encourage new clients to use your service.

Looking good. After you have reached the point where your business is on steady ground and showing increased profits every year, you can afford to dabble in "institutional advertising," as it is called in the trade. This is where you pick up the tab to send a dozen kids to the rodeo when it comes to town, or sponsor a float in the local Fourth of July parade and, in return, get your name listed on the program or on a banner in the parade. This is primarily name recognition only and, while every little bit is helpful, by the time you can afford it, you probably will be in pretty good shape anyway.

Direct Mail

One of the most effective methods of finding subscribers for your newsletter is through direct mail. The phrase may not mean much to you, but you get direct mail pieces all the time. You know those catalogs, brochures or other solicitation materials you get in the mail almost daily from people you've never contacted? That's direct mail.

Since you haven't requested this information, you may throw it away without a second glance. However, if it's an attractive or unusual advertising piece, you probably decide to look it over. Maybe something—a picture or catchy copy—grabs your eye and you order a product from the company that mailed the material.

This is one example of direct mail; unsolicited advertising material which is mailed out to a large group of people. The addressees may be bound by any number of factors—credit card holders, members of an organization, the same ethnic group, age, occupation or zip code. Or maybe they just have the same zip code.

These and the names of people in thousands of other categories are accumulated, organized and sold by mailing-list brokers for use in direct mail campaigns.

There are advantages to using direct mail when starting out, though the cost is too high for most people to use it right off. The primary benefit is control. You can rent a mailing list that is made up of the names and addresses of very specific groups of people.

When you decided on the the subject matter for the newsletter you plan to publish, you most likely had an idea about your ideal customer population. Obviously, if you can reach these potential customers in a focused manner, you will have a greater percentage of people reading your ad materials than if you went with general mass advertising.

Mailing lists can be compiled by you as you gather names, or you can rent/buy them from a list broker. Check in the library for a *Direct Mail List Rate and Data* volume to find brokers in the areas you desire. You will most likely find lists for consumers in your area of expertise and interest.

Designing your Package

What goes into the direct mail package? A letter that is both a handshake to introduce yourself and a sales presentation. It can be a tough balance. Sales letters are the least expensive direct-mail pieces to produce, but they are far from the easiest to write. You may want to hire a copywriter to handle that task for best results.

If you choose to write the letter yourself, bear in mind these points:

- The letter introduces your newsletter to potential buyers.
- It must have a dynamic lead-in sentence.
- It must present crisp and clear information about the benefits of subscribing to the newsletter.
- It must present a feeling of personal communication, written just for the person who's reading it.
- It must be highly professional.

Think of what it takes to draw you into a direct-mail piece and keep you interested until the last word: a thought-provoking phrase in big, bold letters at the top of the page; a simple but thorough explanation of why the letter was being sent and how reading it would be of benefit to you; a direct request to take action; a few testimonials from the service's users; the signature of the company's president. Here is a sample direct mail letter to use as a springboard in writing your own:

How important is your family health?

Dear Friend:

Are you aware of the dangers of giving your child aspirin, especially when they have chicken pox? Are you familiar with an age-old cold remedy that costs pennies and guarantees relief?

Protecting your family against the hundreds of complications which can effect them can be a worrisome task. Everyday we hear of a new flu strain, the life-threatening dangers of blood transfusions, harmful additives in the foods we serve and buy, and more.

Is there a way to keep on top of the latest findings, new treatments and preventative medicine? Yes, there is a way, and it's called *Phase One—Family Health*; a newsletter for concerned citizens.

Every month *Phase One—Family Health* takes a look at developments from research labs, government findings and information provided by private citizens, like yourself, who write to us. We show you simple ageless cures for common problems, like sore throats, acne, and back pain. We give you in-depth details on alternative methods of healthcare, including accupuncture, aromatheraphy and chiropractic.

Take a look at the enclosed sample and see what you've been missing! *Phase One—Family Health* is the newest concept in preparedness and, as you can see, all information is provided in layman's terms with diagrams where applicable and easy-to-follow suggestions.

We'd like the opportunity to show you what we can do for you. To ensure that you do not miss another vital issue, simply fill out the attached form and send a check for $15.95 in the enclosed envelope. Your first issue will be sent immediately.

Don't take your family's health in your own hands. Order today!

Experiment with writing a direct mail letter, get some feedback from friends and associates—perhaps even test it locally—but make sure you're sending out something you *truly* think will work for you. Not all letters will be as focused as the example above, but the elements remain the same.

Include your name and phone number. Shortly after your mailing, make a follow-up phone call if you have phone numbers available. If handled effectively, the combination of direct mail and phone follow-up can generate a great deal of business.

Classified Advertising

Don't underestimate the power of classified ads. Many major corporations utilize the classifieds even though they have sizeable budgets available for display advertising. There are several reasons for this:

1. The classifieds are an extremely reliable testing ground for new products, services and ideas. Although it is true that people who typically "read" the classifieds are a different group from those who scan display ads, they are considered to be responsive and, therefore, can give you a very good idea of whether or not you have placed your ad in the appropriate publication.
2. A short, well-written classified placed in the right publication and under the proper category can be a low-cost method of advertising guaranteeing solid returns.
3. If a company is trying to establish a mailing list, a classified ad that features an "Inquiry" statement, such as "Send name & address for free details (or a brochure)," is a good way to build up a file of qualified buyer's names. And they can be considered qualified buyers because it takes time,

energy and the cost of a postage stamp for them to get your free information. By writing to you they have stated their interest.
4. Classified ads are inexpensive, ranging from 50 cents to $15 per word depending on the publication. With careful planning, you should be able to get broad-based coverage without putting a dent in your operating capital.

Sample Classified Advertisement

> Family health should be a priority. Learn about the latest medical findings, new and old treatments and alternative medical care in *Phase One—Family Health* Newsletter. Send $15.95 for one year subscription to *Phase-One*, Box 123, Anytown, 11111.

Display Advertising

Don't dismiss the possibility of running small display ads, even though they are more expensive than classified advertising, on a periodic basis. Consider offering an incentive, such as a discount or something equally attractive to people who mention seeing the ad. This will give you an opportunity to test the response rate at certain times of the year and will help you in planning future advertising campaigns.

As with classified advertising, it is important to define your market when getting ready to place a display ad. You want to select a publication that will reach the audience you want and then create a specific ad that appeals to that target group.

To Write or Not To Write

Writing display ad copy is not for the inexperienced. Although it is possible to learn how to put ideas and words together that will pull the results you desire, it is recommended that you hire a copywriter if you have any qualms about producing an ad.

However, if you are confident that you can develop your own ad, remember that it must build identity through the use of carefully planned words and design. Glance through newspapers and magazines to find ads that catch your eye. Most likely, the ones that stand out have a memorable logo, effective use of space or an unusual headline that leads you into the body of the ad. These are the ads you should refer to as samples when designing your own. When planning your ad, keep the following elements in mind:

1. *Visibility.* Your ad may well be surrounded by many others, so you must design it so it will immediately attract the reader's attention.
2. *Boldness.* Use large art and/or a bold headline as a focal point.
3. *Simplicity.* Don't overwhelm the reader with too many find details. This is particularly true in a small ad.
4. *White space.* Just because you have, say, a 4 x 6-inch space to work with, it isn't necessary to fill it up with graphics. In fact, white space is a necessary component in assuring your ad will be read.
5. *Use legible typefaces.* The easiest to read are Times Roman and Palatino (the type used in this book), which are known as serif typefaces because of the tiny strokes at the tops and bottoms of the letters. Sanserif (without strokes) types such as Helvetica are okay for ads containing few words, but are difficult for the eye to follow when there is a lot of text. Also, be sure that the type is large enough; generally nothing small than a 10-point type should be used.

Design and Typesetting

It isn't necessary to be a great artist to create an ad, especially these days with the availability of graphic materials, including cut-out and transfer (press-on) letters in different type faces, symbols, borders and design ideas through graphic art supply companies, such as Formatt and Chartpak. Also, most desktop publishing systems (including yours) have computer graphics available that can really dress up your ad at a low cost.

If you feel uncomfortable about laying out your ad so it has eye appeal, consider hiring an art student to handle the job for a prearranged fee or as a school assignment (talk with the head of the art department to see if they have a work/study for credit program). Just be sure to review the student's work prior to making a commitment.

Also, check with the advertising department of the newspaper or magazine you are planning to advertise in. There may be graphic artists or designers on staff who will work on the layout for you. In fact, there still are newspapers in the country that offer full services, from ad concept to design work, at a minimal charge to their advertising clients.

Advertising is the greatest art form
of the 20th Century.

Marshall McLuhan

Publications work on tight deadlines so be sure you start the process early enough to get a proof copy of your ad back in time to make any corrections. You can imagine the anquish in seeing your ad appear . . . with the wrong address. Although the publication would probably do a "make-good" for you and run a corrected ad at no charge, the damage has already been done. The final responsibility for the ad rests on you, so as with any other aspect of your business, plan ahead.

Tracking Ad Response

Some customers will tell you that they saw your ad and might even, if they are the talkative kind, let you know what they liked or disliked about it. They will probably be in the minority, however, so you must develop methods for determining if your advertising is working for you.

One very simple way is to include a coupon for something in the ad and to count the number of coupons you get within a certain test period after the ad runs. There is one major problem with this, however. Even the most well-intentioned people often cut coupons, file them away in a "safe" place and totally forget about them.

So, although you will be able to gauge response to some degree, be aware that many of the people who respond have probably seen the coupon, but simply mislaid it or not the kind of folks who use them.

Predicting Response

There is a standard formula in advertising which provides a barometer for predicting how much response can be expected from either a display or classified ad. The formula states that you will see 1/2 of the total responses from an ad within a certain period of time after receiving your first inquiry or order.

For an ad run in a daily newspaper, the period of time is three days; for a weekly newspaper or magazine, it is six days; within fifteen days for a monthly publication, and within twenty-five days when running in a bi-monthly. Although there will be exceptions to this rule, it does give you a base from which to track response.

Cost Per Thousand (CPM)

The CPM equation helps you develop a cost-effective campaign. Basically, it tells you what your ad cost per 1,000 readers will be. Most publications will provide a CPM comparison upon request (some include it in their Media Kits), but you can easily figure it out for yourself with just a few facts from publications you are exploring as advertising vehicles.

For convenience sake, CPM equations are typically based on the rate of a full-page black and white ad. You simply divide the full-page rate by the thousands of circulation. And it is important that you get the circulation, *not* the readership, for magazines and newspapers typically claim that their readership is two to fifty percent higher because of "pass-along" of the publication to friends or relatives.

For example, if a certain newspaper is charging $2,000 for a full-page ad and they claim their true circulation is 200,000, you will be paying $10 per 1,000 readers for your ad space. Another specialized publication's full-page rate may be $1,000 with a circulation of 50,000. The cost per 1,000 readers will be much higher—$20 per 1,000, but it might be worth it if, for example, you have a unique product or service that is geared to an exclusive market.

Benefits of Paid Circulation

It is also important to know that publications with a paid circulation generally have a readership that is more inclined to respond to advertising. This is because of the simple fact that they are a captive audience who have taken the time to *order* the publication. This is especially valuable if you have a product or service that you are planning to market through mail order channels.

You can find circulation, readership demographics, advertising rates and other important information about a number of publications (especially those with national distribution) through Standard Rate and Data (SR&D) or the Gale Directory of Publications (and their monthly updates), available through the research desk at your local library.

Recently, the Advertising Research Foundation and the Association of Business Publishers conducted a study to determine the impact of advertising on the sale of products.

Several different products were used for the study and each was advertised for a 12-month period in an appropriate publication. The results were interesting, but not surprising to anyone who has ever utilized a solid advertising campaign in promoting their business.

- More advertising meant more sales.
- Determining results from an ad campaign generally took 4 to 6 months. One or two insertions does not indicate viable results.
- Color in advertisements dramatically increased response and, even more important, sales.
- A well-developed ad campaign keeps on working for a year and sometimes even longer in publications with a high "keep" appeal.

Knowledge and belief in your product, faith in yourself and respect for your customers are the keys to succesfully building your future. As you go about starting-up and establishing your business, remember the word "profit." This alone should give you the necessary motivation to get out there and confidently tell the world what you have to offer. ■

21

Promotion and Public Relations

Informing the public about your business through the use of business cards, brochures, mailing pieces, catalogs and specialty items, such as calendars, pens and T-shirts imprinted with your company name, is a form of advertising that is known as promotion.

The things you can do over and above your paid advertising and promotion that help build your image and keep your business in the public consciousness are referred to as public relations. It is a fine line in terminology, but can make or break your business if not addressed.

There are many clever ways to extend the effectiveness of your advertising and promotional dollars, as illustrated in the following examples.

A Little Creativity Goes a Long Way

The owner of a pet grooming business leaves a business card and a brochure featuring a twenty percent discount coupon everywhere he goes. When he is running errands, he always takes a handful of brochures with him to hand to store clerks, gas station attendants and waitpersons he runs into along the way.

If he sees a car with a dog in it, or one with a bumper sticker announcing the owner's affection for their pet, he slips a brochure under the windshield wiper. Does it work? Absolutely. He claims that forty-five percent of his new business is from the recipients of his hand-outs and the majority of them become regular customers.

Another business owner who operates a small walking tour service in her beachside town sends out a one-page quarterly newsletter featuring historical and other facts about the area to everyone who has ever taken the tour. She includes a $10 coupon which can be redeemed by former clients or their guests.

She states that many of her clients are local residents who send their out-of-town visitors on her walking tour, simply because she makes sure they are aware that she is still in business and generates enthusiasm through the newsletter.

Advertisements contain the only truths to be relied on in a newspaper.

Thomas Jefferson

"Thoughtful" Promotions

Other ideas you might consider include promoting humanitarian outreach. For example, for every ten products a customer buys or every tenth use of your service, you donate a predetermined amount of money to a local charity. You can easily keep track of their purchases by punching a hole at the edge of a card designed by you or your printer strictly for that purpose.

When you are ready to present the check to the particular charity, make sure the chairperson of the organization is going to be available to accept it and be sure to contact the local press and invite them to the "event." In most cases, they will give you free coverage.

According to successful entrepreneurs, free give-aways are the most successful promotional gimmicks. You can order specialty advertising items, such as pens, notepads, calendars and hundreds of other items, with your name and phone number printed on them as give-aways. Every time the recipient uses the item, they automatically think of you! Check under "Advertising-Specialty" in the yellow pages for prices and ideas. ■

22

Resources

Associations

Advertising Research Foundation
Three E. 54th Street
New York, NY 10022
(212) 751–5656

Association of Business Publishers
205 E. 42nd Street
New York, NY 10017
(212) 661–6360

Newsletter Association
1401 Wilson Blvd., Suite 402
Arlington, VA 22209
(703) 527–2333

General Reference Books & Periodicals

A Consumer's Guide to Telephone Service. Consumer Information Center, Pueblo, CO 81009.

Bacon's Publicity Checker. R. H. Bacon and Company, Chicago, IL. (A comprehensive listing of major newspapers in the United States and Canada.)

Brownstone, David M., and Gorton Carruth. *Where to Find Business Information.* New York, NY. Wiley-Interscience, 1982.

Encyclopedia of Business Information Sources. Gale Resource Company, Detroit, MI.

National Five-Digit Zip code and Post Office Directory. U.S. Postal Service, Address Information Systems Division, 6060 Primacy Parkway, Memphis, TN 38188.

National Trade and Professional Associations of the United States. Columbia Books, Inc., Washington, DC.

Roget's International Thesaurus. New York, NY. Harper & Row, 1977.

Superintendent of Documents, Government Printing Office, Washington, DC 20402 (Request listing of publications).

Tax Guide for Small Businesses. Internal Revenue Service, Washington, DC. (Available through your local I.R.S. office; request publication 334.)

Ulrich's International Periodicals Directory. R. R. Bowker and Company, New York, NY.

Webster's Ninth New Collegiate Dictionary. Springfield, MA. Merriam-Webster Inc., 1983.

Small Business Associations & Government Agencies

American Marketing Association, 250 South Wacker Drive, Chicago, IL 60606-5819 (Marketing publications available to non-members).

The Association for Electronic Cottagers, P.O. Box 1738, Davis, CA 95617.

Bureau of the Census, Washington, DC 20233 (Statistical data).

Copyright Office, Library of Congress, 101 Independence Ave. SE, Washington, DC 20559 (Information on copyrighting written and visual materials).

Council of Better Business Bureaus, 1515 Wilson Blvd., Arlington, VA 22209 (Ask for a listing of their "Booklets on Wise Buying").

The Dun & Bradstreet Corporation, 299 Park Avenue, New York, NY 10171.

International Franchise Association, 1350 New York Ave. NW, Ste 900, Washington, DC 20005 (Regulation and information on franchises).

Minority Business Development Agency, Office of Public Affairs, Department of Commerce, Washington, DC 20230.

National Association for the Self-Employed, 2324 Gravel Road, Fort Worth, TX 76118.

National Association of Women Business Owners, 600 South Federal St., Ste 400, Chicago, IL 60605.

National Federation of Independent Business, 150 West 20th Ave. San Mateo, CA 94403.

National Insurance Consumers Organization, 344 Commerce Street, Alexandria, VA 22314 (Send self-addressed stamped envelope for free booklet, "Buyer's Guide to Insurance").

National Minority Business Council, Inc., 235 East 42 St., New York, NY 10017 (Quarterly newsletter for small and minority businesses).

National Small Business United, 1155 15th St. NW, Washington, DC 20005 (Send for info on federal legislation for small businesses).

National Trade and Professional Associations of the United States, available through the research desk at your local library.

Occupational Safety and Health Administration (OSHA), Department of Labor, Washington, DC 20210 (Employment regulations).

Office of Information and Public Affairs, U.S. Department of Labor, 200 Constitution Ave. NW, Washington, DC 20210 (Request publications list regarding employment).

Patent and Trademark Office, Commissioner, Washington, DC 20231 (Details on applying for a patent).

Small Business Administration, 1441 L Street NW, Washington, DC 20416 (For booklets and information on the Service Corps of Retired Executives—SCORE). ■

Index